the
Thin Line
Between
Cupcake
and
BITCH

We as women underestimate ourselves. I'm pretty smart. I work pretty hard. I'm pretty good at what I do. I have really good instincts. I have great ideas. And I can execute. I say that out loud because we as women don't pat ourselves on the back. We're always sort of deferring. We cede our power so easily.

—Michelle Obama

Joni Wickham

with Teresa Bruns Sosinski

the
Thin Line
Between
Cupcake
— and —
BITCH

Taking Action, Driving Change,
Getting Results

Requests for permission should be addressed to: Ascend Books, LLC, Attn: Rights and Permissions Department, 7221 West 79th Street, Suite 206, Overland Park, KS 66204

First Edition
10 9 8 7 6 5 4 3 2 1

ISBN: print book 978-1-7323447-8-5

Library of Congress Control Number: 2019956476

Publisher: Bob Snodgrass
Editor: Jennifer McDaniel
Publication Coordinator: Molly Gore
Sales and Marketing: Lenny Cohen
Dust Jacket, Book Design, and Illustrations: Rob Peters
Cover Photo: Paul Andrews Photography, paulandrewsphotography.com

Printed in Canada

www.ascendbooks.com

To my daughter, Vivian, and her big sisters, Emily and Libby. I want you, and every woman who reads this book, to see yourself as a leader. Define "leader" in whatever way creates the best personal and professional fulfillment for you. But whatever, whoever, and wherever you lead, do it with all your heart. And in the process, if you are ever underestimated, don't become bitter. Be better.

—J.W.

Contents

* Includes Top Ten Leadership Lessons

Foreword

*J*oni Wickham is nice, helpful, charming, and delightful. She is also assertive, ambitious, competitive, and accomplished. Women walk a tightrope between being seen as overly feminine (likable, but not competent), or overly masculine (competent, but not well liked). In order to get ahead, women are expected to be both – and this tension can put them at a disadvantage as they face pushback for the very behavior that's admired in their male colleagues. This dynamic must change. *The Thin Line Between Cupcake and Bitch* serves to do just that.

Based on her repertoire of personal and professional experiences, Joni shines a light on the tough transition women must make to succeed in what has traditionally been a man's world. Joni takes a powerful approach to creating the positive change our operating systems require. She is all the things a good leader should be – and funny to boot.

Throughout her career, and as you will read in her book, Joni has demonstrated vision and purpose, commitment and passion, emotional intelligence, empathy, resilience. She has also shown creativity and innovation, transparency, confidence, and above all, honesty and integrity. The book affords its readers great lessons in leadership while remaining very funny and quite compelling. I'd venture to say, it's "edutaining."

I highly recommend every woman interested in a successful career in what is currently a man's world – and every woman interested in combating the status quo ensuring equity in the workplace – read this book. It's fabulous!

Susan C. Freeman
CEO, Freeman Means Business

Introduction

"*G*AWD! **What in** the hell do you need with more school? You need to just get a job like the rest of us."

That was it. That was the moment I decided once and for all that I'd have to leave the home and community in which I was raised, and some of the people in it, in order to have the life and impact on the world around me that I was seeking.

My cousin fired those words off at me during a family get together at the rural North Carolina home of my mother's parents, Grandma and Grandpa Peterson. Their home is a quaint doublewide trailer, which always struck me as being very "homey" despite how modest it was. Home is home, I suppose, even when what you consider your home can be pulled down a street on wheels. It was at that moment, as my cousin finished her silly thought, when I decided I was done with apologizing for wanting a life different than the one I was born into. This wasn't the first time I heard and felt the low bar of mediocre expectations other people had set for where they thought my life should go. It didn't bother me if I didn't get invited to a classmate's birthday party because I was what they described as a "trailer rat." But I felt dejected and frustrated when people automatically had low expectations of me because of where I came from.

To say I've had to learn to straddle two different worlds may be an understatement. I was born to a fifteen-year-old girl whose parents never finished high school, but I managed to earn a master's degree. My grandparents on both sides were major influences in my life, even if at times they didn't understand what I wanted to do with myself. None of them were educated beyond elementary or middle school, but they all taught me some important life lessons that – like the value of a strong work ethic – that have been important tools in my toolbox.

During my childhood, my father's parents, Grandma and Grandpa Chamblee, lived in an old farmhouse with tobacco fields all around. The house sat beneath several large oak trees at the end of a long, dirt road. Even as recently as the mid-1980s, we used an outhouse because there was no operating bathroom inside the house. My grandpa set up a big bucket with a padded seat to use in the middle of the night. But sometimes there was no option but to walk the 25 feet from the front door and use the outhouse. This also meant the very real possibility of running into all sorts of wildlife like guineas, foxes, raccoons, and my least favorite of all – black snakes. Those snakes were so big from eating the mice living in the tobacco barns that when they slithered out on the limbs of the oak tree, they would eventually fall off on whatever or whoever was below. I can remember being four or five years old and running as fast as I could to the outhouse in the middle of the night. I was so scared because I didn't want the snakes dropping onto me like in a horror movie. It's a big reason why I'm irrationally scared of snakes today.

But those snakes also served as a cautionary tale. Grandpa Chamblee would tell me, "Those snakes ate every mouse they could because nothing stood in their way. The snakes were bigger and stronger than any mouse. Don't be like those snakes. One day when you're big and strong you need to be sure you're helping people around you, not just taking advantage of them because you can."

Grandpa Chamblee had a sixth-grade education, but he was wise beyond the number of years he sat at his school desk. In the spring and summer, he and I would walk down that dirt road in front of their house and find honeysuckle. He'd catch me staring at the highway in the distance when we got to the end of the dirt road. "Girl, you were born to take that highway out of here," he said. "But that day isn't today. Slow down." I guess he knew I wasn't going to follow in the footsteps of most everyone he had known. I was not staying to work on a farm, in a factory, or at a restaurant. Instead, I had my heart set on shaking up the decision-making table a bit. Even though I didn't have a vocabulary to match my understanding at that point in my young life, I had seen the impact government, public policy and politics could have on the working poor – especially women – and most of the time it wasn't pretty. Clearly, I didn't come from a politically connected family, so I had no idea how I was going to get a role in shaping decisions. I knew how to work hard so I assumed that was a good place to start.

So, how can someone with such a modest background write a book about women in leadership positions? I quickly learned that a large dose of work ethic certainly helped, but a good education, a streak of stubbornness and resiliency, a dedicated tribe to show you the way, and a sense of humor were requirements as well. The stories in this book illustrate ways I navigated issues and situations. Some are "down-home" stories – like being the first person in my family to ever purchase a business suit for a job interview. Others are more serious, like overcoming gender and socio-economic biases, and why I hope to help women – and men – change their perspective on women's leadership.

I may have my "feminist card" revoked for this, but I believe that including men is just as important as including women in our efforts to build and support women leaders. My journey includes an amazing group of women who pushed me to maximize my potential, but men have also recognized that potential, mentored me and given me a chance to shine. Part of leadership is, and always will be, the ability to bring people together. Enlisting more men in the fight for gender equity is not only necessary, but smart.

This book also provides a roadmap for women to consider when pondering what their personal and professional journeys might look like. Beating impostor syndrome, redefining social norms, leveraging emotional intelligence, and leading through conflict are all important considerations for women leaders. These are all areas for men to reflect on, too, because women will get where we need to be quicker if the other half of the population is in this fight with us.

My story isn't complete yet. At the end of 2019 I concluded my time as Chief of Staff for Kansas City, Missouri Mayor Sly James. He and I started Wickham James Strategies & Solutions, a consulting firm, after term limits prohibited him from running for reelection. This chapter of life seems like a good time to share a few insights I've gleaned through my personal and professional journeys. Admittedly, I've screwed up a few things, but there are lessons to be learned there as well. I don't pretend to have all the answers on how one should navigate childhood poverty, gender discrimination, and other societal ills. But I am hopeful this book will be helpful and, if nothing else, serve as a reminder that sometimes you have to laugh to keep from crying – or punching someone.

And, yes, in case you are wondering, there is a thin line between Cupcake and Bitch.

Chapter 1
Words You *Don't* Want to Hear from an Elected Official

*T*here I was – nineteen-years-old, a freshman at Meredith College, an all-women's college in Raleigh, North Carolina, and ready to make an impact on the world. All I needed was a chance to show those folks in those power positions that I had potential. I was going to prove that I wasn't really a trailer rat.

I'd set my heart on landing a great internship for a United States Senator and had an interview appointment. I found myself sitting in the reception area with two other interviewees, one female and one male. Each were well-dressed with a nice briefcase. The woman was blonde, had on a navy suit and wore a large pearl necklace. The pearls were so big I was afraid her neck might break from their weight. From where I sat, she looked miserable as if that was the last place on Earth she wanted to be. The guy was average looking, with nothing discernably interesting about him at all. His appearance made me think that someone had advised him to dress so that he didn't bring any attention to himself. It seemed to me that both applicants were accompanied by their professors. Or at least that's what I assumed.

I was the beneficiary of mentoring from one of my professors, too. She was a political science professor at Meredith College who had taken an interest in me and watched me as I navigated professional life through a bit of trial and error. When I told her about my interview for the Senator's campaign, she had the foresight to ask what I planned to wear. I'll never forget the look on her face when I told her I was going to check out Men's Wearhouse for a good deal and then have my grandma alter it. At that point, I had no idea that women wore different types of business suits than men. They all looked equally foreign to me. She told me to be at her office that evening and the two of us would go to Belk, a popular department store in the Southeast, because I needed to learn how to shop for women's business attire. I kept that suit in my closet for over a decade as another reminder of a lesson this trailer rat had to learn.

I understood that my mentoring relationship with my professor was an exception, so I couldn't figure out why these students interviewing for the internship would bring professors. "Who does that?" I asked myself incredulously.

Since I was the last candidate scheduled for an interview, I watched and listened as the Senator's staff person greeted the other applicants and their professors. As I listened, it didn't take me long to realize these weren't college professors, but the fathers of the applicants. Oh, and they were major political donors.

God bless the Senator's aide who interviewed me when it was my turn. She was kind enough to be fairly engaged during the interview, although we knew this was a waste of time for both of us. I didn't come from a politically connected family. I'm pretty sure I even have a couple family members who can't vote because of their criminal histories. And no one I knew had a dime to donate to a political campaign.

I drove to my Grandma and Grandpa Chamblee's house after the interview feeling demoralized, crushed, and angry. I worked so hard on my resume and cover letter. My advisor told me it was the best cover letter he had ever read. I had prepped for that interview for over a week. Bought a suit. Washed my hair and even put on those stupid fake nails that prevent any sort of use of your hands.

My grandpa was sitting on the swing outside when I drove up, and he could tell from the expression on my face that it didn't go well. I told him all about what had happened. I expected him to be indignant on my behalf. Instead, he said, "Well, driving out here mad at the world isn't going to do one thing to get you that job." He didn't know what an internship was, so he just referred to it as a job. He told me if I was going to give up the first time someone shut a door in my face then I probably wasn't cut out for "politicking" anyway.

"The first time you drove a tractor you backed it into a fence," he said. "The next day I fixed the fence, and you got back on the tractor and figured out how to work the gears."

I am usually not the sensitive type, but one thing that always hurt my heart was the thought of disappointing one of my grandparents. I shook my head and helped with chores before driving back to Raleigh for classes the next day.

That day was the first time in my life that I ever skipped class. I went to my mailbox when I returned to campus from my grandparents' house and inside was my *College Democrats* newsletter. I read that the Senator I desperately wanted to work for was having a fundraiser at a judge's home who lived only about 20 minutes from campus. Maybe this was my chance. If they saw how hard I was willing to work, then perhaps they'd give me an opportunity. I'd be the most hardworking volunteer they'd ever seen.

I drove to the judge's home, where I found a lawn maintenance crew preparing the yard and setting up the large, white tents – a clear sign that something fancy was about to go down. I helped with the tent. I raked the leaves. I set up tables and decorated them. I set up chairs. And I even mended a broken podium with a bottle of wood glue I found in the glove box of my car. I had no clue how it got there, but I was thankful for its existence. I did all these things as a volunteer while many of the politician's paid staff stood around watching the activity. Two of the onlookers were the intern candidates whose fathers accompanied them on their interviews just the day before.

It was my lucky day. A senior staffer, who was taking media calls, saw what I was up to. She hired me on the spot to be a communications assistant. Not an intern. A paid, part-time job. She told me she needed a hard worker on her team who would do whatever it took to get the job done. It was obvious that my two competitors for that internship didn't actually like working all that much.

I was over-the-moon about my new gig. I felt I could see where that highway at the end of the dirt road at the Chamblee house would take me. I couldn't wait to tell my family about this opportunity I worked so hard to get. I called my mom and stepfather to tell them first.

My mom deserves so much credit for working hard to lift us out of poverty. She graduated from high school – the first in her family to do so – despite being encouraged to drop out once she found out she was pregnant with me. While in school she worked multiple jobs, including long shifts at a barbeque restaurant serving eastern North Carolina barbeque and sweet tea. She had a strong vision for where her life, and mine, should be headed and stuck to her guns without much support or direction. My biological father has never been a big part of my life, but we're making progress now that I'm old enough to realize how short life is, and how futile it is to try and change people.

My mom and stepfather married when I was in second grade. My stepfather, a retired dentist, treated me like his own child from the beginning of his courtship with my mom. He is thirty years older than my mom, and it's fair to say that he has always held traditional views on gender roles.

Neither my mom nor my stepfather was politically active. At that point in time, both were dismissive towards politics and government, and it should have been no surprise to me that they were less than interested in this internship. Their main concern was that I get a degree in a field where I could support myself. My stepfather suggested that maybe I save my interest in politics for a hobby during elections. This was a pretty underwhelming response to something I worked so hard for. I hung up the phone and called Grandma and Grandpa Peterson.

My Grandma Peterson woke up every day at 4 a.m. for over twenty years to work at Hardee's and make biscuits. Ironically, she is the worst cook I've ever met. Probably because she knows only a few sight words and she's not able to read many recipes. Grandpa

Peterson worked several factory jobs on the assembly line over the years. I have vivid memories of him telling me about his work making street sweepers at the former Athey Products plant in Raleigh.

Grandma and Grandpa Peterson are salt-of-the-earth and they love me dearly. They helped take care of me while my mom worked from the time I was born until my mom and stepfather married and we moved about an hour and a half away. Despite how different we are, I value the opportunities I have to travel back to North Carolina and stay with them in their quaint, homey trailer. It keeps me humble and driven at the same time and gives my daughter, Vivian, a well-rounded perspective on life when we visit them.

But, when it comes to education and career, Grandma and Grandpa Peterson don't see things the way I do. The experience of landing this job in the Senator's office was the first time I felt that in a real and painful way. When I told them what had happened and that I had got a job after all, they seemed almost insulted. "Why can't you just be like everybody else?" Grandma Peterson said. "Are you too good to work at a restaurant?" For her, an office job was for lazy folks who couldn't handle "real" work involving manual labor or making food for a living. Grandpa Peterson was surprised that I wanted the job because he thought the Senator's staff obviously preferred rich kids.

I had no idea how to explain this situation to them in a way that didn't come off as dismissive or defensive. I didn't even try. In fact, I changed the subject to NASCAR. It was the first of many times that I tried to summon the emotional intelligence to find common ground in a difficult situation. The way I saw it then and still see it today: you have to meet people where they are. When I told my girlfriends what had happened with my Grandma and Grandpa Peterson, they couldn't believe I had backed down so easily. My grandparents were genuinely content in their trailer with their elementary school education and worldview, so that's where I kept things with them. That experience continues to shape my interactions with them, but I've learned over time not to let it deter my vision for where I want to go.

I had struck out twice telling my family about this new job with the Senator, so next I called Grandma and Grandpa Chamblee. Besides farming the acreage around the house, Grandpa Chamblee worked at a rock quarry for decades, rarely missing a day and never complaining about the grueling manual labor. My Grandma Chamblee was a saint for dealing with my father's temper. She held a couple of factory jobs after raising her children and late in life went to work flipping burgers and making coleslaw at a local hamburger joint.

Like the Petersons, they also had elementary educations. But unlike the Petersons, they understood that I wanted to do something different with my life. They loved the idea of their only grandchild getting an education, supporting herself, and pursuing a fulfilling career. I have many memories of reading the newspaper to them so they would know what was happening in their small community. They struggled with reading skills, but that didn't mean they didn't care about the world around them. We would play cards and watch the news at night together because there was no money for trips to museums, movie theaters, or dance classes. Those Sunday mornings before church we spent watching David Brinkley helped shape my outlook and probably piqued my interest in politics, government and the media.

Grandpa Chamblee answered the phone like he always did with his signature, "Go ahead," rather than "Hello." He was an avid deer hunter and his CB radio was his version of today's iPhone. Hunters used the greeting "go ahead" when they were called on the CB. He was dedicated to deer hunting because the perfect shot meant meals for the family. It wasn't about taxidermy for us.

After I told him all about being hired in the Senator's office after the disappointing interview situation, he paused only long enough to spit out the juice from his wad of chewing tobacco. "You done good, girl. You done good." He called my Grandma Chamblee to the phone, and she started warning me to make sure I kept my grades up while I worked because, "You've got a head full of sense, and you need to use it." But I could tell she was just as pleased as Grandpa.

After processing my family's varied reactions, I felt like I was finally on my way. In some respects, I felt like I was already halfway there. Little did I know, I still had so much to learn and so many gaps to fill – everything from resiliency and self-confidence to how to handle other people's low expectations of me. There was much to overcome – like learning some general dining etiquette.

A couple weeks after I started working in the Senator's office, I attended my first political fundraiser. I was asked to follow him while he worked the room and to keep track of all the business cards collected from donors that evening. Before dinner I had been a bit relieved when I saw a young man, about my age, who was setting the table. He seemed to me to be even more out of his element than I was. I thought I'd take pity on him and help him collect the extra plates that I assumed he mistakenly put on the table. "Who the hell needs four plates on a dinner table?" I thought to myself, and I was positive the bus boy didn't know what he was doing. How was I to know that some people had the audacity to purposefully dirty more dishes than needed just so they could have a different plate for salad, bread, the entrée and dessert? Well, I learned so that evening after embarrassing myself in front of the state's political elite. In a poetic turn of events, it was the bus boy who enlightened me on the proper way to set a table.

That night when I sat down for dinner with eight of the richest people in North Carolina Democratic politics, I was so nervous I couldn't eat a thing. Not that I would anyway since I didn't know what the tiny glob of meat on my plate was. I was certain it wasn't chicken tenders, and therefore, it didn't interest me. But I did know to keep my dinner roll on its own plate.

Working for the Senator was filled with experiences I never thought I'd have. Representing an agricultural state like North Carolina, a tobacco or cotton field is a good optic for a press

conference. So, I set up press conferences in fields that looked just
like the ones I'd played in as a child. Eastern North Carolina soil
boasts lots of red clay, which is often used for baseball fields. While
I can see how that red clay is helpful to keep a baseball field intact,
it is extremely hard to dig the holes necessary for tent stakes. But
we got the tents up so the attendees would have some protection
from the sun. And dry, red clay was preferable to prancing around
in the mud created by unpredictable rainstorms.

Next, we had to figure out how to get people from their cars
to the folding chairs under the tent. This is where I learned the
lesson about stiletto heels in mud. Women who attended the event
in stilettos were miserable as they walked on their tip toes to their
seats. There is a time and a place for everything, and a cotton field
is not the place for stiletto heels. As the people in suits took their
seats, I was asked to run into the nearby fields and ask the farmers
to stop their loud farm equipment until the press conference ended.
This was a difficult ask for me because I understood very well how
precious every minute of sunlight is for people who make a living
in agriculture. But the Senator needed it to happen, so I took off
running through the fields chasing Massey Ferguson plows and
John Deere tractors. The farmers did stop their work long enough
for the press conference, and the Senator gave his speech with the
sleeves on his white-collared shirt rolled up.

It wasn't lost on me at the time and it still feels true today: the
juxtaposition of standing in that red clay surrounded by cotton
or tobacco plants while watching the democratic process unfold
was a bit surreal. I was witnessing my childhood and small-town
upbringing intersecting with my professional life. It wouldn't be
the last time that I felt the small-town girl inside me.

It was also during this time that I first experienced the
significance of power and government from an inside view. Growing
up, I saw my grandparents interact with government bureaucracy
when applying for farm subsidies, food stamps, or unemployment.
I stood in line at the health department with my mom for health

care because we couldn't afford the doctor's office downtown. But now – even as a part-time staff member for a Senator – I was in a position to help efforts to increase funding for farm subsidies and break down barriers to accessing food stamps and health care. Through some of my communication work, I was able to channel the power of the Senator's office to help raise awareness of federal funding for the Women, Infant and Children's Program (WIC). At the time, it was an underused program in rural North Carolina primarily because the government wasn't communicating well, or at all, with the families who needed it the most. You can't use a program if you don't even know it exists.

While working on these issues, I became the "go-to" writer when something needed be whipped out quickly. I've always been able to write fairly well and quickly. Maybe the genesis of that skill was following Grandpa Chamblee through the fields of tobacco and cotton and writing down what his plan was for each row. I always wondered how he managed to remember the plans before I was old enough to write them down for him.

As I was approaching the end of my freshman year in college, the Communications Director asked me to write a speech for the Senator. The speech would be short, but she hammered home how important it could be. The Senator had caught the eye of national Democratic party leaders and, if we played our cards right, he might be a presidential candidate sooner rather than later. This task made me so nervous that I ran to the bathroom twice to throw up while I was writing it. I can't even remember the topic of the speech now. But what I can certainly remember is being petrified of screwing it up and ruining this chance to show that I could deliver when the team needed me most.

I pulled myself together to draft the speech and turned it in by the deadline. All that was left at this point was to wait and see if the Senator liked it.

Up until then, I had few personal interactions with the Senator. Imagine the terror that went through my bones when one of his top aides came to my tiny cubicle to tell me that the Senator wanted to speak with me. I was certain I bombed the speech and would be fired.

With my palms sweating and heart pounding, I walked into his office. The Senator didn't even look up from what he was writing. "Take a seat. I'll be with you in a moment," he said. Because his voice was tired and stressed, I was convinced I had written an awful speech. Now I realize that elected officials are oftentimes just stressed with the weight of their responsibilities.

As he walked over to the couch I was sitting on, I could feel tears welling up in my eyes. He sat down beside me and looked me right in the eye, like all the good politicians do.

"Joni, we don't know each other well, do we?" he asked.

"No sir," I responded thinking at any minute I would burst into tears. But I was absolutely determined not to cry.

"Well, in spite of that, I want to tell you something that I think might help you in the long run," he said.

What followed was a profound moment for me both personally and professionally. He spent a solid five minutes telling me how good the speech was, and how I was a better writer than people on his staff who were not just older than me, but had more education, experience and confidence.

The Senator then told me that I would often be underestimated because I was a petite female with a southern accent, who's "kinda cute." He told me that these things might cause some people to see me as not as smart as they were, and some would even think I didn't belong at all because I couldn't possibly know what I was talking about.

And then the Senator said something that has stuck with me even today. He said, "You can be bitter and pissed at the world because of people underestimating you, or you can figure out how to use it to your advantage. It's 100 percent up to you."

When we walked out of his office, the Senator told me again how great the speech was. Except this time, it was in front of his top three advisors – all of whom were balding, white males. Their expressions told me that everything the Senator had just told me was true. They had underestimated me and didn't expect my speech to be worth a damn.

I drove back to campus in a complete fog. It's surprising that I didn't run off the road when I was driving down the crowded beltline in Raleigh during rush hour. I was trying to process the advice I just received from a U.S. Senator. He said it was advice, but in that moment, it felt more condescending than helpful. I felt many times in my nineteen years that I was underestimated because of my upbringing and socio-economic status. The Senator was now telling me that it was my appearance that could also cause people to underestimate me.

I shared this story with a couple of friends that night. One thought I should have slapped him and that I was too nice to him. The other told me to just ignore what he said altogether because he was probably just hitting on me anyway.

I went to my professor who had helped me find the suit for the interview and told her what the Senator said. I could tell by the look on her face that his "advice" struck a chord with her. She encouraged me to take some time to reflect not so much on the words he used, but on his message. I replayed his words in my head: "You can be bitter and pissed at the world because of people underestimating you, or you can figure out how to use it to your advantage. It's 100 percent up to you." What was the Senator's message?

That spring of my freshman year, I began running, not so much for the exercise, but to clear my head and manage my thoughts about everything in life. I still run. Usually alone and not wearing headphones so I can think. It's truly therapeutic for me to be alone with my thoughts. After a few days and a couple of runs thinking over – and over – the Senator's advice, I decided that he told me precisely what I needed to hear, even though I certainly didn't want to hear it. His lesson: it was up to me how I would react when someone underestimated me because of my appearance or my background. Just getting angry about it wouldn't change anything and it wouldn't help me reach my goals.

If he had taken more time to explain, it may not have hit me as hard as it did. What I first heard was, "no matter what you do, you're going to be underestimated" and it was a bit of a shock to have someone with power and influence tell me that I'd likely be faced with reacting to perceptions rather than shaping them. Hopefully, his advice has done more to empower me to be able to shape people's perceptions of me, rather than react.

What I later came to understand was that people could see me as too nice like a "cupcake." Or they could see me as too aggressive, a "bitch." I had already experienced this dynamic a bit, but how was it going to determine the way I worked?

I can see now, with twenty years of experience in my rearview mirror, that he'd given me a gift. He was warning me that I needed to learn to manage my reactions when I felt I was being underestimated. For me, being underestimated has never been a matter of "if," but "when."

Chapter 2
Well, *Bless* Your Heart!

One of my high school English teachers assigned us a paper and I worked on it for weeks. I was just beginning to develop a passion for writing, and I loved the process of putting together a good story. I was called to the principal's office a few days after I turned in my paper and found my English teacher waiting for me. She was accusing me of plagiarism. Somehow, she just couldn't believe I was capable of being *that* good of a writer. She knew where I came from, so how could I be talented at anything other than flipping burgers?

I told Grandma Chamblee what my English teacher had told me. "Bless your heart," she said as she gave me a big hug. "But, she's the one with the problem – not you."

If you've ever spent time in the South, you know that "bless your heart" can have several different meanings depending on the speaker's intent. There's the warm and fuzzy definition that translates to "I'm so sorry that you're going through this." That's how Grandma Chamblee meant it when I told her what my teacher said. She was showing me sympathy and included a side of righteous indignation.

There's the "duh" definition of "bless your heart" which roughly translates to "Wow, how can you be so dumb?" This version is usually accompanied by an eye roll, a deep sigh or hands on hips – and sometimes you get all three. At other times, you'll hear "bless your heart" when a rough situation arises where the person is clearly out of their league.

Finally, there's the "I am so over you that I am quietly plotting your demise" definition. You better watch out if you're the object here. Ostensibly, you've done something forbidden and will be shown the door.

Looking at my professional journey from the outside, I would say that I've fallen into the "Wow, how can you be so dumb?" category of "bless your heart" quite a few times. This is what happens when you find yourself being the first to venture out of the mold everyone else around you fits into. Gaffes, mistakes or faux pas – whatever you want to call them – I'm guilty of committing my share.

I still have those "bless your heart" moments and probably always will. I believe that we need to continuously fill the gaps in our knowledge and experience. But there are also times when you just have to find the humor in tough situations. Sometimes I have decided to laugh off a snide comment to avoid going for the perpetrator's jugular. That strategy has come in handy from time-to-time when someone underestimates my contributions to a situation.

I never knew how poor we were until I went to kindergarten. Up until that time, everyone I knew lived the same way we did. But in kindergarten, I remember the kids making fun of my clothes and how I was the only student in the class who didn't get invited to Molly Tucker's birthday party. I'm sure her parents didn't want the trailer rat in their house. I suppose Mrs. Tucker also took issue with me taking up "perfectly good space," in a select group of my classmates who were given the opportunity for beginning Spanish lessons. From Mrs. Tucker's perspective, I was someone who lived in a trailer and would always live in a trailer. So, why bother with broadening my horizons or investing in my education? I'm not sure Molly understood why I wasn't invited to her party, but I did. This is one of the earliest experiences where my assumption that I *will* be underestimated rather than I *could* be underestimated, all began.

This dynamic of being marked as underprivileged, and therefore not worthy of academic opportunities, persisted throughout much of my formal education in my hometown. Stereotypes and biases are hard to shake anywhere, but I believe they are more pronounced when you're living in a small town. At the very least, it's difficult to escape those stereotypes and biases, even for a minute, when everyone knows everything about everybody. For some people, if they don't know your business then they'll make it up. And for others, trying to understand people or issues they have had no exposure to, can feel like a rejection of everything they've known.

While working in the mayor's office, it wasn't unusual for me to visit my Grandma and Grandpa Peterson's house – the trailer in the field—and my Grandma Chamblee en route to business meetings on the East Coast. I try to pack a lot into my trips home to North Carolina. I help the Petersons however I can when I'm with them, whether it's with paperwork or yardwork. My Grandma Chamblee was by then in an assisted-living facility, and so I try making up for living so far away when I visit by filling her room with the basics like snacks, toiletries, and new socks. Grandpa Chamblee passed away, so my biological father is the only local person who's left to care for her. Doing my part isn't always easy from Kansas City, so I tend to go into "overdrive" as Grandpa Chamblee would have called it, when I'm physically present. Whatever time is left I spend visiting old friends from high school and occasionally catching up with a couple of professors at Meredith College. When my daughter, Vivian, travels to North Carolina with me, we also try to visit as many people as possible – both friends and family – so she can get to know the people who helped shape my views, outlook, and experiences. I don't want her to be sheltered and close-minded. I've told my husband, Fred, that it's important to me that she is as comfortable running around a tobacco field as she is going to summer art camp at Kansas City's Nelson-Atkins Museum of Art.

A few years ago, I stayed with my grandparents for a couple of days before heading to Washington D.C., for the winter meeting of the U.S. Conference of Mayors with Mayor Sly James. When I arrived at Grandma and Grandpa's trailer, a pot-bellied pig was running around their backyard. Deer, coyotes, and turkeys are common sights in their backyard, but the pot-bellied pig was a smelly intruder, and no one had any idea how it got there. We assumed it got loose from a nearby farm and was just wandering around finding the Peterson homestead a nice place to visit. Quite annoyingly, it followed us everywhere and tried to jump in the car every time we left the house.

The morning I left for Washington, D.C. to join Sly, the pot-bellied pig kept jumping all over me when I was in the yard helping Grandpa rake leaves. The pig was now not only smelly, he had also found a nice mud puddle to roll around in. Grandpa and I raked the leaves into manageable piles for him to burn later that evening, and the pig did his best to get in our way.

When it was time to leave for the airport, I went inside to put on a suit. Since there wasn't time to change at the hotel before the meeting, I had to make the short flight from Raleigh ready to go to the White House. There I was inside the trailer I had practically grown up in, putting on makeup and curling my hair for a meeting at the White House, while a stinky, muddy, pot-bellied pig ran around outside. In that moment, my life epitomized the textbook example of a dichotomy.

While I was putting my luggage into the trunk of the car, the pig jumped on me several times and I kept trying to shoo it away. "He's just being friendly," Grandma laughed. Traffic on the way to the airport was bumper to bumper, and I made a mad dash through security and to the gate to make my flight. I was exhausted by the time I landed in D.C. After my visits to North Carolina, my physical and emotional energies have usually taken a hit.

Despite being tired, I knew I had to be "on" that evening when I arrived at the White House. I dropped my luggage off at the hotel without time to touch up my makeup or catch my breath. In less than a few hours, I had made the shift from my family life at a trailer in North Carolina to walking into the White House as Chief of Staff to the Mayor of Kansas City.

That evening was simply unforgettable. If I was dreaming, then I didn't want to wake up. President Barack Obama exuded his typical charisma while he greeted every guest who entered the room. He never seemed tired of shaking hands or making small talk, and then he delivered a rousing speech about bipartisanship and the need for leaders in D.C. to act more like mayors – pragmatic and results-driven. Several members of his cabinet were there as well, including David Agnew, Deputy Assistant to the President and Director of Intergovernmental Affairs. David is a kind soul who embodies servant leadership and immediately made me feel right at home at the most well-known address in the United States. Sly and I spoke with other mayors and their chiefs of staff about everything from gun violence to pensions. Also, I never get tired of hearing leaders from other cities rave about Kansas City.

When the reception ended, we looked for the correct exit to catch a cab on Pennsylvania Avenue. But somehow, we walked out the wrong door and were on the wrong side of the White House from where we needed to be. Realizing our mistake, we tried to walk back inside the same door we had just exited. Bad idea. The Secret Service, with their weapons by their sides, started yelling, "No re-entry! No re-entry!" Long story short, we managed to get in a cab without being arrested and ending up as a front-page headline in the *Kansas City Star*. I started my day chased by a smelly, muddy pig and ended it with members of the Secret Service shouting orders at me. Dichotomy.

In contrast to the high-profile speeches about healthcare reform and climate change, I couldn't help but think about where I was when the day began for me back in North Carolina. My grandparents were now probably sitting in their living room recliners watching TV. Perhaps Grandma had already washed the towels and sheets I had used, and Grandpa had switched over to decaf coffee in the hope he might be able to sleep a little bit. On the other hand, I spent the evening mingling in the Rose Garden, inadvertently provoking the Secret Service, and taking in the sights of D.C.

When I returned to my hotel room, I was still thinking about the juxtaposition of my day – and President Obama's cool factor – when I noticed something on the pants leg of my red power suit. It was mud. Not just a small smear, but lots of it. I had gone to a reception at the White House with pig mud on my suit pants.

If Grandma Chamblee had been there, I'm sure she would have said, "Bless your heart," with a whole bunch of sympathy.

It can be emotionally taxing to confront the effects of a poor education and poverty on a regular basis. I have been able to see the injustice right in front of my eyes and how it affects people I love. Many aspects of life, ranging from healthcare to economic mobility, are complex in this environment.

Grandma Chamblee had a debilitating stroke in 2008 and became paralyzed on one side of her body. She could no longer live alone so we started exploring assisted-living options while she recovered from brain surgery. The assisted-living facility estimated the cost of her living there would be about $6,000 per month. Finding an assisted living facility in 2008 that didn't feel like something from the 1970s Soviet Union was eye-opening. I found myself trying to explain government regulations and processes to the rest of my family when we were forced to sell her trailer in accordance with Medicaid requirements. This trailer was not the Taj Mahal. It had plumbing issues that were so pronounced that rusty water came out of the pipes when either the bathtub or kitchen sink were used. Grandma had stopped washing white clothes in the washing machine because they would turn orange from the rust. The trailer also had a hole in the kitchen floor, patched with plywood. This home only sold for about $650, but Medicaid required that she have no assets when she entered the assisted-living facility, so there really was no choice. Trying to sell that nearly worthless trailer and everything in it while coping with Grandma's stroke and her decline, felt inhumane. That entire experience showed me something that I knew from my work in the Missouri State Capitol, but now understood in a very personal way: this country's healthcare system is cruel and punishes the poor and undereducated.

There are benefits to my modest background that have only become clearer to me as I get older. The contrast from my upbringing in a small, rural North Carolina town to an adult life in a metropolitan city as a government official means that sometimes I don't have a sense of belonging to either group. But it also means that I've experienced different ways of life and perspectives, which is not a bad thing at all.

I've mentioned that I don't always have much in common with some of my family in North Carolina, but I also can't completely relate to colleagues who can borrow start-up capital from their family or who come from a long line of heavy-hitting political donors. I can see that many people operate in their own little bubble. It's easy for someone with little exposure to others who are different from them to be judgmental. I've seen this often, even from those you least expect it.

Throughout 2018 I participated in the Greater Missouri Leadership Foundation's women's leadership program. Established in the early 1980s in Texas by then Governor Ann Richards, the program sought out women who had the expertise and experience to serve on boards and commissions. Doing so proved to be more difficult than Richards anticipated, so she initiated a leadership program to train women in areas of leadership, community engagement, and public policy. Southwestern Bell, a Texas-based company, was an initial sponsor of the program. When Southwestern Bell relocated employees to St. Louis, those workers who attended the Texas leadership program, in turn, started the Greater Missouri Leadership Foundation. The Foundation's goal is to bring together women from across the state and from a variety of professional backgrounds to network, build leadership skills, and prepare themselves to serve their communities in some capacity. It's an amazing organization that does so much to help women leaders.

Before serving on the Foundation's board, I participated in one of the leadership sessions in Kirksville, a small town in northeast Missouri that's home to Truman State University. About 25 women participating in the program were joined by a panel of four women who worked in agriculture. During the panel discussion, one of the women – a farmer – talked about her day, which typically began around 5 a.m. and involved a lot of planning around Missouri's temperamental weather patterns. She remarked how she couldn't imagine living "in the city where everyone has to drive an hour each direction every day." Many of us "city girls" just looked at each other. Of course, not everyone who lives in a city drives an hour to get to work. Other assumptions about city lifestyles included how our neighborhoods must be riddled with crime and that we never see our kids because we worked outside the home. Educating to erase these stereotypes is why this type of leadership organization exist – to broaden the horizons of the participants and the panelists through dialogue and interaction.

It's always been striking to me how easy it is for people to rush to the wrong conclusions and inaccurate judgments when they make little to no effort to learn about how other people live. Missouri politicos talk a lot about the "rural/urban divide." That divide doesn't exist just in Missouri and it doesn't only exist between rural dwellers and urbanites. There is a real division between most socio-economic classes. That divide has contributed to the rise of populism and anti-intellectualism that's so present in our country today.

My family and friends in North Carolina had preconceived notions about what my life was like. One family member is always happy to let me pay when we get together for breakfast during my trips home because, "You did all that school, so I bet you're loaded now!" This comment is without regard to the fact that yes, I went to college, and I have the college debt to prove it. I look forward to the day when someone else in my family goes to college, so they can share the assumption that they're loaded and take his or her turn picking up the tab for everyone.

It's also surprising to see how some of my friends and colleagues I've met in my professional life can't relate to people and situations outside their own experiences. It's typical for someone who has never stepped foot on a farm to assume that farmers are less sophisticated businessmen and women than individuals who wear a suit to work each day. In fact, many farmers have technical and scientific expertise including GPS tracking on farm equipment and computer programs tracing the growth of each row of crops. Without a sophisticated business acumen and a nuanced understanding of plant science and meteorology, our country's food system would be dramatically different. I also have friendships with individuals who admit that they've never had a meaningful relationship with anyone from a more modest background. I've had to debunk the myth that there is a correlation between poor people and laziness. Other times, there is almost a sense of confusion about how the lower end of the socio-economic ladder lives.

Several years ago, I was Christmas shopping with a friend, and she asked me what was on my list. I told her that I was buying a present that my grandparents would give to Vivian. My friend was surprised that Grandma and Grandpa weren't buying the presents themselves. From my friend's perspective, it would be fun for them to go shopping for Christmas presents for their only great-grandchild. I gently explained that they would absolutely love to do that, but both of them had recently retired from low-wage jobs and the small retirement nest egg they had managed to save didn't allow for many items outside the basics. My friend seemed surprised that for some retirees, the extra expense of buying gifts was beyond their reach. In her experience, those sorts of expenses were included in a financial forecast prepared by a financial planner. That was not the case for my hardworking grandparents who were relieved to just get by.

Considering all of these dynamics, and the fact that I am acutely aware of two different ways of life – one that involves a professional career and financial stability, and one that is reflective of generational poverty and a lack of educational opportunities – it does sometimes feel like I'm on an island without many people who understand my frame of reference. I have been on the side of "bless your heart" many times when I've operated in unfamiliar territory and proved that I had a lot of catching up to do. Plus, I'm frequently "too fancy now" for a lot of people I grew up with.

It is what it is. But I try to be authentic no matter what kind of room I'm in or who's in it. Authenticity is a freeing trait that's hard to argue with.

I've not always felt comfortable in my own skin, but I've noticed that has changed as my confidence has grown. I now shudder to think of the days when I was absolutely determined to take speech lessons and lose my southern accent. My assumption was that when people heard me talk, they would automatically think I had a low IQ. A former boss told me my accent meant I was better able to grab someone's attention when I spoke. Shedding that concern about my accent even led me to pursue speaking engagements on topics like gender bias and offering political commentary on television.

I began to see that who I was and where I came from was a strength and not a weakness, and it could be healthy for me and perhaps inspire others. I could help build bridges between different types of people because I have one foot in a world built around the American dream and the other foot in a world where getting by while living paycheck to paycheck is the definition of success. Although difficult at times, my childhood prepared me to take action, drive change and get results. Today, I'm a woman who is well suited to work on public policy issues and public relations campaigns aimed at lifting women and children out of poverty. I know how to communicate with families who, like members of my own family, are relieved just to be getting by. I understand firsthand the dilemma of choosing between food on the table or paying the electric bill. I saw my grandparents and mother tackling those same challenges.

Grandpa Chamblee embodied honesty. He taught me that all

forms of honesty were critical but not as rooted in daily interactions as they should be. Grandpa would not do business with anyone who was dishonest in their work. Once, while we waited for work to be completed on his old pickup truck, we overheard a mechanic telling a coworker about overcharging a woman for tires. "She didn't know how much they were supposed to be anyway!" the mechanic sneered. When the mechanic finished talking, Grandpa asked him how he'd feel if someone did that to his mother. Grandpa must have made his point because the mechanic called the woman back and told her that a "mistake" was made on her bill and she could pick up a check for the difference that afternoon. Grandpa never went back to that mechanic. He considered dishonesty a telling description of someone's character, and if he felt that someone was dishonest with him, then he had no use for their company or patronizing their business. Grandpa would say, "Dishonesty sucks away trust like a tick on a dog."

When I first showed an interest in politics, Grandpa Chamblee warned me about dishonest politicians. He admitted he didn't know much about politics but didn't feel like it would matter if he did. In his view, politicians said whatever it took to get elected and stay in office.

Grandpa's life was disconnected from the hustle and bustle of North Carolina's state capital in Raleigh. He would sometimes talk about going to town when he was younger but only to sell tobacco and cotton. By the time I was in college, the only time he went to town was for medical appointments. Similarly, the Outer Banks of North Carolina with its beautiful views were only a four-hour car ride from where he and Grandma Chamblee lived, but I could never get him to ride with me to the beach. He ended up dying without ever seeing the ocean.

He may not have traveled or seen the democratic process up close, but Grandpa understood the value of keeping your word whether you're working on a political compromise, closing a business deal, or just promising to show up to bale hay. This emphasis on honesty has stayed with me through the years. In the early days of my career, I can remember when Democrats and Republicans would fight like hell and disagree all day long on political issues and votes. But by evening, they would grab a drink together and talk about anything except public policy. Those moments together built relationships much deeper than political parties, and those relationships were built on trust and honesty.

Today, Grandpa Chamblee's lessons on honesty are even more astute because it seems like politics is focused more on transactions and less on relationships. At the risk of sounding like a traditionalist, I think the impersonal "gotcha" nature of social media and term limits, which reduce the bench of self-actualized leaders on both sides of the aisle, contribute to this. Perhaps there is something to be learned about the art of the deal from an old farmer. If you repeatedly go back on your word, you might just find yourself short of allies when you need them the most.

My personal experience in such vastly different ways of life makes me reflective at times. I've realized that there are some constants no matter what someone's frame of reference may be. Most people have a desire for safety, good health, and prosperity – it's how those things happen or don't happen that shapes us. Where we came from doesn't have to determine how far we can go. At the same time, using our past to teach us lessons in humility, resiliency, hard work, and honesty can help us travel roads that can be bumpy and crooked. In some cases, perhaps the best starting point is a gift to remind us of the work that still needs to be done.

Chapter 3
Country Dumb

*L*ike many professions, politics has its own lingo. Campaign staffers, for example, talk a lot about "favorables," which refers to a candidate's particular set of personality traits or achievements that can be sold to voters. In the Missouri Senate, it's becoming more common to see someone running down the hallway mumbling, "They're going to PQ!" This refers to the infamous "previous question," which is a way to cut off debate and force a Senate vote. "PQing" a bill typically angers minority party members and statehouse reporters and is viewed as a way to shut down discussion on contentious issues.

Getting my start in politics in the South exposed me to some regionalized political lingo as well. I can remember reporters from outside the region looking at each other with blank faces when they'd hear a phrase like, "He's burning slam up on the trail!" which means the candidate is really connecting with voters. Another phrase frequently used was, "He doesn't have the sense God gave a billy goat," the meaning of which was easier to uncover but reporters never wanted to use it as a direct quote. There's something about referencing a billy goat to illustrate a political candidate's intelligence that seems less than sophisticated to some, I guess.

I've learned lessons in leadership from observing these political sayings in action as well as watching how other people lead. Sometimes learning what NOT to do is even more important than seeing a productive leadership style modeled. Strategy, continuous learning, resiliency and discernment are some leadership qualities reflected in interactions throughout my own journey. Those qualities are critical regardless of your background or industry. Leaders often face situations where a multi-faceted strategy requires learning new information, being resilient when everything doesn't go as planned the first time and discerning top priorities from tangential issues. Each of these qualities is important on its own, but the most effective leaders combine them.

My favorite expression I learned while I was still in college and a paid intern for the North Carolina Senator was, "Just go in there and play 'country dumb.'" This refers to a situation when you are very well aware of what's going on, but it's not to your advantage to admit it or show it. To someone on the opposing side, you may appear unsophisticated, or even dumb. But, in reality, you are putting up a screen or camouflage to gain an advantage, and the opposition underestimates you. You're being strategic about how you use information and relationships to achieve your goals. This is usually a strategy that works best when used sparingly.

I observed a North Carolina state legislator negotiating a bill to regulate pesticides with executives from the tobacco industry. The tobacco industry said publicly that, in the spirit of compromise, it was working on a variety of agreement points so that the bill would pass swiftly. Tobacco companies wanted the public to think they were interested in reducing the toxins they had been adding to the environment. But privately, tobacco executives did not want any provisions of the bill to pass. They were working hard to torpedo the bill by conjuring up scare tactics about job losses if these pesticide safeguards were to pass. The tobacco industry believed that more stringent regulations would increase production costs and decrease profits. Its plan was to blame the legislator for the bill's demise by accusing him of being too obstinate to forge any consensus. There are just some people who make things more complicated than they need to be. Rather than having a direct conversation with the legislator about their concerns, the tobacco industry preferred playing political games. For anyone like me who grew up with such an emphasis on honesty from my grandparents, this was difficult to watch from the sidelines.

What the tobacco industry executives didn't count on was that the legislator was well aware of their plot. He could have called them out and made a spectacle of the situation. But instead, he continued about his business, collecting the votes he needed by working with advocates who wanted to see the industry regulated. In the end, the tobacco industry lost its fight. The bill was passed and the safeguards on pesticides became the law. The Senator had been closely watching the efforts of the state legislator and observed, "Tobacco guys don't have a clue what's coming at them." Using the "country dumb" approach worked for that legislator. He was strategic in working with advocates on the bill despite the odds. He knew the tobacco industry had a ton of money to use against him. He also knew they'd paint him as not pragmatic enough to represent his district's farming community. But what they didn't expect was the state lawmaker understood their strategy and that his "country dumb" strategy would prevail.

In 2017, the "country dumb" tactic showed up again in Kansas City while I was Sly's chief of staff. Sly and our City Manager, Troy Schulte, set out to pass an $800-million infrastructure bond, the largest in Kansas City's history. It was important to allocate a substantial amount of funding for sidewalks because the crumbling, or even nonexistent sidewalks, were a constant issue for residents. The $800-million bond may sound like a lot of money, but it doesn't take long to allocate every penny of it when a city the size of Kansas City actually has more than $2 billion worth of infrastructure needs. One city councilman was particularly difficult during negotiations on the spending allocations. He wanted more money spent on roads. He pointed to complaints from residents about the condition of our roads as his basis for throwing an oversized chunk of money in that direction. Yet, several of us knew he had a tendency of opposing or dismantling everything Sly tried to accomplish. I suspected that factor weighed more heavily on his mind than the actual complaints about road conditions.

Like the tobacco industry executives, this councilman made it impossible to have an honest conversation. He was the type Grandpa Chamblee had no time for. I sat in meetings with him negotiating what this infrastructure package would look like knowing the whole time what his real priorities and intentions were. "Country dumb" came in handy here because it helped me summon the patience to sit in a room with political games being played. In order to prove our stance, the Mayor's office collected hundreds of signatures from residents in the councilman's district who signed a petition demanding sidewalks. The councilman's protests against sidewalks soon stopped after that. Maybe his commitment to his original public policy stance had waned. Or maybe this experience taught him something about the views of his constituents, and he was more concerned about their opinion of him rather than being an obstructionist. Perhaps a little bit of each option was at play.

This situation reminded me of one of the Senator's observations: What differentiates good politicians from bad ones is their ability to play "country dumb" in political negotiations without looking stupid to their constituents. What a balancing act.

My personal background, combined with a lack of political connections and experience, plus that gender bias toward a petite female with a southern accent, has often resulted in my feeling out of place. I have felt unprepared and not "country dumb," but actually dumb. While some people have gaps in their understanding of certain subjects or skills, I've often felt mine were more like craters. This is where mentors can help fill in the blanks. Mentors are important relationships for anyone to cultivate and nurture but are particularly critical for those of us who don't naturally have a strong professional network. Though I lacked material items and certain life experiences during my childhood, I've hit the jackpot when it comes to men and women who have mentored me in my professional life.

When my undergraduate degree was completed, I moved to Missouri to get a master's degree in political science from the University of Missouri. After immersing myself in Missouri politics working for a teachers' union, I got a job with Missouri Secretary of State, Robin Carnahan. She showed me what grace under pressure looked like every time she walked the halls of the Missouri State Capitol. Robin was the daughter of Governor Mel Carnahan, who died in a plane crash with his son and a longtime advisor in October 2000. When he died, Governor Carnahan was running for the U.S. Senate against Republican incumbent John Ashcroft. Missouri voters posthumously elected Governor Carnahan to the Senate. His wife, Jean, a remarkable leader in her own right, was appointed to fill his Senate seat. Republicans in the Missouri General Assembly must have still been embarrassed by this loss when Robin was first elected Secretary of State in 2004 because at times, they seemed focused on stopping her political career. Those halls were full of men looking for any reason to criticize her every move and decision. Later in my career, someone on the Mayor's office staff asked me how I learned to "operate like a ninja" under extreme stress. I learned from watching Robin be herself at the State Capitol. She never lost her poise and professionalism, even while being grilled in public hearings by men with half her expertise and experience.

Those men, including Democrats, often criticized Robin for being "emotionless." This felt like code for "She's so bitchy!" Robin was the first high-profile female leader I closely worked with, and I could plainly see gender bias showing up in how she was perceived by legislators and the media. If it bothered her, she never let it show.

A strong mentor relationship can sometimes help you in ways you can't predict. Robin and I have kept in contact through the years, but we don't talk every week or even every month. But in the fall of 2019, she was one of the first people I wanted to talk to when I found a lump in my breast. I was waiting to hear the biopsy results from the doctors, but I had dozens of questions that they just couldn't answer. Robin had battled breast cancer in 2006, so I knew she'd understand the rollercoaster of emotions. Her diagnosis came shortly after being elected Secretary of State. She had to fight for her health while juggling an important new role – all under the watchful eye of the media and the public.

I knew Robin would have some answers. But what I didn't expect was her level of concern and warmth for me. I texted her and she called me within five minutes. We talked for more than an hour. My list of questions was long: What if this tumor was cancerous? How was I going to tell my six-year-old daughter? The news hit my husband – who is twenty years older than me – very hard. We already assumed the cycle of life would look a certain way, but what if this changed everything? Grandpa Peterson had recently been diagnosed with colon cancer. If I had cancer, should I even tell him, or would he be better off focusing on his own fight? Sly and I had just launched our consulting firm a few weeks earlier, and that was weighing on my mind, too. How would I be able to pull my weight in the business if I had to undergo chemo or radiation?

In pure Robin fashion, she had a well-considered answer for everything. She had encouragement and advice about potential treatment that put me at ease. She reminded me that I couldn't take care of everyone else if I didn't take care of myself. When I hung up the phone, I thought if Robin was able to fight this battle so publicly and so soon after being elected Secretary of State, then, once again, I should follow her lead.

There is never a good time for a cancer scare and that's particularly true when trying to get a new business off the ground as well as navigate the health insurance industry while newly self-employed. But Robin was instrumental in focusing my attention on what was most important – my health and my family. Most of all, she assured me that no matter how the pathology came back on the tumor, I would be fine. Hearing the confidence in her voice was exactly what I needed. Her mentorship had never been more important to me. This was the ultimate lesson in prioritizing values and resiliency. The experience also showed me how fragile life was and that we were all better off focusing on the people and things that bring us joy.

The biopsy came back benign, and no further treatment was necessary after the lumpectomy. Still, I have to be vigilant with self-exams and sonograms and mammograms every six months.

Another mentor, Mindy Mazur, who was Robin's Chief of Staff when I was hired, saw something in me during my interview for a position on Robin's team. I had a piece of paper proving I had the education and qualifications, but unlike many of my colleagues, I didn't have any political connections at the Missouri State Capitol. I've often wondered what made her give me a shot. Maybe she saw my tenacity. Mindy gave me assignments on critical issues like voter protection and engagement. These assignments gave me a platform to showcase my ability to not only digest, but also to communicate complex public policy issues under tight deadlines and intense scrutiny. And to my surprise, I was even able to build relationships across the aisle to help pass legislation.

It was that role that started to alter my trajectory. Who knew my humble roots in rural North Carolina would be an asset to me when I was trying to find common ground with Republican legislators from Missouri's Bootheel? I found that my understanding of life in rural America, and of the values held close by many rural voters, helped me when I had to make a case for specific public policies. That frame of reference was beneficial when I needed to make the case for implementing early voting, and when I had to educate legislators across rural Missouri about the negative consequences of requiring a photo ID at the polls. I had to convince rural legislators – most of whom were white, male, and Republican – that increasing access to voting across the state, not limiting access, was good for democracy and their districts in rural Missouri. In the end, we got early voting further through the legislative process than we expected and fended off photo ID while Robin was in office.

The position with the Secretary of State's Office connected me to Larry Jacob and Amy Jordan Wooden. They had worked on Sly James' first mayoral election in 2011 and were on the Mayor-Elect's Transition Team, looking to fill his staff. I had no experience in Kansas City politics, but, once again, Larry and Amy must have seen "that something" that I didn't see at the time. They asked me to meet with Sly that spring, and I joined his staff just after his inauguration.

After eight years of closely working with Sly – most of that time serving as his Chief of Staff – I could fill a whole book with "Sly-isms." One such "Sly-ism" is, "Don't be hyperbolic!" But it isn't hyperbolic for me to say that meeting him was life changing.

Mentorship and sponsorship are different. Mentorship happens when one person guides another through his or her journey while providing insights, feedback and coaching. Something magical happens when both the mentor and the mentee improve their skills and professional status through the mentorship. Sponsorship brings the relationship to a different level. A sponsor proactively elevates the work or stature of someone who is less accomplished or subordinate within an organization or system. And when the stars align, that certain someone might just summon the courage to write a book about her journey, launch a consulting firm and kick impostor syndrome to the curb – for the most part.

Sly James is my ultimate sponsor.

Watching him in a leadership role showed me that being completely at ease with who you are and where you come from is freeing. Authenticity is hard to come by in some circles, politics certainly being one. Working by his side grew my confidence because his worldview and decision-making were genuine, and he always seemed so comfortable in his own skin. He consistently put the city above his own political interests. Watching his leadership style, I often thought, "If he can do that in this way, then I can, too." If that isn't leadership, then I don't know what is.

The dynamic between an elected official and his or her Chief of

Staff must be built on trust and mutual respect. I've seen instances where neither of those qualities were present and it didn't end well. A Chief of Staff must be a thought partner to an elected official. Being a thought partner can sometimes mean telling them what they do not want to hear. Other times, it means knowing them well enough to know that you need to be their opposite. Sly admits that he's usually the engine and I'm the brakes. His demeanor is well-suited for an executive role, like mayor. He is a bold decision-maker and is undeterred by push back. But sometimes even the strongest executive needs someone by his side who can finesse relationships and manage the political deal-making that comes with the territory. That was usually me. On a few occasions, it was helpful for me to lean into the Cupcake role when he was in a hard-nosed mindset.

The most profound and public example of Sly's sponsorship for me came in 2013. I was simultaneously very pregnant and very busy coordinating an important meeting between Kansas City's development community and the labor unions. I did one-on-one briefings with all parties involved so that I could relay all the divergent perspectives to the Mayor. I also took the time to develop trust with each stakeholder so they would understand the Mayor's objectives for the meeting before we even walked into the room. I spent hours working with each of the participants, and it didn't go unnoticed. The CEO of one of the participating economic development organizations commented, "I can't believe you can still work this hard with your stomach that big!" My knee jerk reaction was to roll my eyes – or worse. I'll never be able to fully explain why I didn't react aggressively. Maybe it was the amount of naivete in his tone, or the size of my ankles that day, but I just laughed and said, "Thanks."

When we arrived at the board room on the day of the meeting, I couldn't believe what I found. No one had included a chair for me at the table. There sat eleven men in their seats with their name cards sitting in front of them. Sly's chair was at the head of the conference table, but I literally did not have a seat at the table for the meeting I had solely planned. I had researched, analyzed and briefed the Mayor and participants on issues, and even reserved the conference room. Bless their hearts.

Sly has an ability to make a strategic spectacle when he needs to. And he did. He made all the participants move their chairs to create a space for me at the table next to him. He then went to the corner of the room where the extra chairs were stacked and sat down one for me. Sly had a few harsh words for the group, but I don't recall exactly what he said. Those men treated me differently after that incident. But it took another man with power they wanted to leverage acting as my sponsor in order to make it happen. Without question, I had earned my place at that table, but Sly made sure they knew it. I'm certain that I exhibited much more of a bitch vibe than cupcake vibe throughout that meeting. In that moment, it was important for those guys to know that I found their omission completely unacceptable.

Examples like this illustrate how important men can be in efforts to combat gender bias and discrimination. It would be one thing for me to take on the behavior of those eleven men by myself. But Sly's willingness to step up and call them out created more urgency and perhaps a stronger sense of shame. There is also a domino effect that can come when enlightened men stand up for women. One of the men at that meeting told me a couple of years later how he recently advocated for a woman in his company because Sly's point made such an impact on him. Sometimes the best way to take action, drive change and get results is to change the attitudes of the people around you. Men have just as much responsibility to dismantle gendered stereotypes as women.

In addition to mentors and sponsors, continuous learning can also help fill in the gaps. I have often felt like I lived in a smaller world than many of my friends, peers and colleagues. My suitemates at Meredith College couldn't believe I was a college freshman before I had ever set foot in an art museum. I studied abroad in Russia my last year at Meredith, and it took me a while to figure out how to call home because I didn't know what a country code was for a phone number. More recently, Sly taught me the proper way to hold a wine glass. Continuous learning is just that – continuous.

I've worked hard to avoid falling into the trap of stagnation in terms of personal and professional growth. Just because "country dumb" is a real thing practiced in certain situations doesn't mean "dumb" is an adjective to describe some level of incompetence. "Country dumb" is a strategy for personal and professional interactions, not a commentary on intellectual capacity.

Learning both social and professional skills that didn't come naturally to me, or that weren't honed earlier in my life and career, has broadened my horizons and increased my confidence. The staff who worked in the Mayor's office can vouch for my obsession with leadership development. Early in my career, I thought leadership was a skill only a select few individuals at the top of the food chain had or even needed. Later, after observing outstanding leaders and some who had no business leading anything, I decided it was time to reframe my view about leadership. I made sure to enroll in organizational leadership classes when I was completing my master's degree. I've also made a point to consistently seek out seminars and trainings to learn the latest trends and concepts in leadership.

Gallup's Clifton StrengthsFinder, a talent assessment tool, should be required reading for anyone who works in groups or leads groups. My own personal and professional experiences are proof that sometimes someone else needs to see your leadership potential before you recognize it yourself. With this in mind, I've tried to expose colleagues to leadership concepts. I particularly want to provide leadership training to young women who are more prone to impostor syndrome – that sinking feeling that you're just not good enough.

The same is true for gaps in or lack of personal experiences. Not everyone is born into a family where exposure to museums and ballet is common in childhood. For some of us, those experiences don't come until well into adulthood. I was working on the student newspaper in college and the staff was pulling an all-nighter to make sure the *Meredith Herald* was the epitome of journalistic integrity – at least in our humble opinion. I was sent on a mission to get coffee for us and was asked to order a coffee drink I'd never heard of – a latte. It seems like such a small thing now, but I can vividly remember the experience.

I had never ventured into a coffee shop before. There wasn't even one in the entire county where I grew up. So, my experience with coffee ranged from the instant coffee we drank to keep warm and alert in a deer stand during hunting season to the weak, but bitter, stuff at Hardee's. Putting as much effort into coffee as a barista was not something I was familiar with.

But thanks to the detailed instructions from my friends, I managed to order the lattes without any major hiccups. I was a bit surprised at how long it took to make a latte. I couldn't imagine my grandparents waiting in line so long for a fancy coffee drink. I wasn't brave enough to try a latte that day, so I stuck with my usual order: black – no cream, no sugar.

Later that week, I told Grandma and Grandpa Chamblee and Grandma and Grandpa Peterson about the latte and the coffee shop. "Is your mama spending all that money to send you to that school so you can learn about shit like this?" Grandma Peterson retorted. She's still not a fan of lattes. As usual, Grandpa Chamblee's response was more measured. "Well, at least you're learning how different people live," he said as he spit his Red Man chewing tobacco into his spit cup.

The contrast in how people live their lives has always been striking to me. Some people feel at home ordering a latte at a coffee shop while others prefer instant coffee from a thermos in a deer stand. While we all experience life differently, what's most important is that we make attempts to understand each other. Maybe if we did more of that, our political system could be geared towards action and results and not partisan arguing.

Traits like resiliency and discernment can be learned anywhere – in a trailer park, on a farm, on Pennsylvania Avenue, or at City Hall. No matter our frame of reference or what we're trying to accomplish, leaders who keep moving forward in the face of adversity – and those who can wisely discern and prioritize goals – will achieve results quicker than others.

Resiliency is a job requirement in politics. People who aren't resilient and who can't pivot quickly when dynamics change don't make it very long in the everchanging political world.

The history around Kansas City's efforts to build a new single terminal airport is proof of this. Soon after Sly took office, it became even more apparent that our city couldn't maximize its potential without reimagining Kansas City International Airport. The three-terminal configuration built in the early 1970s was outdated in terms of security and was highly inefficient for the modern traveler. The travel experience was so bad at the airport that even the airlines were hesitant to add flights to and from Kansas City. They were concerned if travelers had a bad experience at any of the terminals, they'd blame the airline and not the airport.

This created an issue for the city and Sly's administration from an economic development standpoint. It was difficult to convince companies considering Kansas City as a possible location for their headquarters that the airport could meet their travel needs. The airport's shortcomings were also painfully obvious when we tried to win the bid for the 2016 Republican National Convention. One RNC official told Sly that he loved Kansas City, but we absolutely had to do something about the decrepit airport.

Voters can surprise even the most-seasoned politician from time to time. Their affinity – or lack of – for inanimate objects like an airport can be so intense that you'd think a life was on the line. In one of our earliest polls, only about 26 percent of voters agreed with us that KCI needed to change. One huge issue we had to overcome was getting voters to understand that the airlines and not the taxpayers would be paying for the new terminal.

Very rarely does an elected official take on an issue when an overwhelming majority of voters oppose it. But to those of us working to bring more opportunities to our city, we knew we had no choice but to figure out a way to get the job done. The years that transpired were a true test of resiliency, full of misperceptions, political drama, and intense campaigning.

At one public hearing the aviation director basically told the audience, which included the local media and City Council members, that Kansas City was going to get a new airport whether they liked it or not. That didn't help anything. Next, a citizens' task force examined the issue for months, ultimately determining the current configuration of the airport was not meeting the city's needs. However, voter appetite, determined by our polling data, still disapproved of building a new airport. A new City Council was elected in the spring of 2015, and several new council members were opposed to a new single terminal – and almost everything else the Sly James administration tried to accomplish. This opposition presented additional complications to putting the issue on the November 2016 ballot. In the spring of 2016, the airlines themselves – the group that would actually pay for the new terminal – finally went public with their strong desire for a new terminal. However, Sly had to put the campaign for a new single terminal on hold because new polling showed we needed more time to convince public opinion on the issue. At that time, less than 40 percent of voters favored the new single terminal concept. It would've been risky to have the public vote when such an overwhelming number of voters needed convincing.

This was the first time while working at City Hall that I felt like we might not be able to accomplish an important goal. Part of me wanted to give the opposition the middle finger. I have no doubts that a few select City Council members saw more of my inner bitch come out during this time. I didn't have much patience for my cupcake side. Eventually, I realized that if I was going to be the Mayor's thought partner and collaborator on this problem and lead our staff through such a bumpy moment in our administration, then I had to be resilient and focus on the job at hand and not the behavior of a few people more interested in creating drama than opportunities to move the city forward. It was clear we had to prioritize goals, and so we focused on the $800-million infrastructure bond first and pressed the pause button on the airport terminal.

The funny thing about resiliency is that it's contagious. The people around you are more likely to get up, dust themselves off and try to solve a problem a different way if they see their leaders setting that example in front of them.

We turned our attention to the infrastructure initiative, but never lost sight of the airport dilemma. While we were working on getting the bond passed, we teamed up with the business and civic leaders, the experts at the aviation department, and neighborhood leaders to educate voters on the need for a new single terminal. Sly said that if two people were gathered and wanted to talk about the airport then he'd go talk to them, and he meant it. It also meant I'd do the very same thing.

One political consultant in town advised me to drop the issue and convince Sly to move on to other priorities. But this was also the same person who had been such a pill to work with on other campaigns that we decided not to use his "help" on the airport issue. He also warned me I would be ruining my career and Sly's if I didn't listen to his advice. After all, he argued, he'd been at this a lot longer than I had and knew better than I did about the limitations in moving public opinion.

What he didn't know was that we had good reason to believe that our voter-education efforts were paying off. During our conversations where he had mistakenly offered what he considered to be guidance; I'd just give him a blank stare. All the while I remembered that sometimes the wisest move you can make is to play "country dumb." We knew voter appetite was shifting, but that wasn't his business. Despite that fact, he'd tell potential campaign donors that we didn't know what we were doing. He'd also leak misinformation to the local media, which fueled the fires some antagonistic City Council members fanned to log jam our efforts. His modus operandi was to create drama so he could position himself as the only person who could fix the problem. Rather than rewarding his bad behavior by giving him a role on the campaign, we stuck to our strategy and ignored him as much as we could.

On November 7, 2017, 76 percent Kansas City voters approved a new single terminal. In the end, our resiliency had finally paid off.

Discernment was one of the lessons I learned while growing up in the rural American South. Grandma and Grandpa Chamblee knew they were uneducated and were reminded of it every single day. But they also valued what a good education could do for me and my future. I can't recall a single toy they ever bought me. But I do remember the books my grandma would bring home when she would go to town with her friends on Saturday mornings. Sometimes when you can't afford much, you can truly discern what is actually important. That's when you learn to make decisions based on needs and not wants. Grandma and Grandpa saw the need for a good education.

We found out Grandpa Chamblee had terminal cancer about a month before I was supposed to leave for Russia. I cried more than I think I'd ever cried in my life and swore I wouldn't leave. I told him I would stay and take care of him and make sure Grandma would be OK. I could travel another time.

But he wouldn't have it. He told me he hadn't worked to help raise me just to be the reason I didn't experience the opportunities right in front of me. He wasn't an educated man, and he never traveled, but he could discern a lot about life and happiness. He was alive the day I came home from Russia and listened as I told all my stories about traveling the world and seeing things he couldn't fathom. I told him all about Red Square, the Russian ballet and, of course, the vodka. He saw my pictures, and we talked and laughed about all my adventures. He died three days later.

Resiliency and discernment are certainly two key ingredients to using the "country dumb" approach effectively. Both are also vital to the leader who can guide people and organizations through tough times. It's easy to be a leader when things are rosy, but not so much when you feel like you're constantly fighting a multi-front war. Leading is also difficult when you feel like you're being underestimated or treated unfairly.

The term "country dumb" rubs some people the wrong way. I can understand why, if you've never seen it in action, or used it yourself as a strategy to get results. It can be a method to get valuable information or to gain credibility with different groups. Sometimes, it's just a good way to build relationships and listen to a different perspective. Many times, trial and error has been the only strategy I've had to navigate a sticky situation. In these cases, the "country dumb" approach is an asset because I have the ability to turn those low expectations into an advantage.

Speaking of country dumb, those tobacco executives had the gall to show up at the bill-signing they worked so hard against. I overheard one of them say to the North Carolina state legislator, "We never really had a chance, and you knew it the whole time."

"True," the state lawmaker said.

He outwitted them by playing "country dumb."

Chapter 4
Complaints or Action: Only *One* Will Get Results

My **patience runs** thin with persistent complainers. It's difficult to be around people who would rather stew in their own frustration than find a solution or take action to improve the situation. Maybe that's because I can still hear Grandpa Chamblee's voice saying, "Some people enjoy complaining almost as much as they enjoy doing nothing about it."

When any staff member came into my City Hall office to complain about the bureaucracy of city government – or that something wasn't going the way he or she thought it should – my response was always, "So, what are you going to do about it?" We'd talk over the problem and discuss possible solutions, turning their frustrations into action.

Taking effective action against gender bias is not always easy. Being on the receiving end of demeaning behavior is exhausting and repeatedly facing gender bias can turn even the most upbeat woman into a person mired in pessimism and anger. But staying angry or looking negatively at the world rarely helps any situation. It not only weighs you down, but also inhibits your most effective leadership qualities from shining through.

We probably all know people who often seem overwhelmingly mad and bitter. Even if we might have some compassion for why they act the way they do, we still find them difficult to be around. These people have what I call "mad-at-the-world disorder." They find certain situations and issues maddening but usually don't make any effort to change things. You may also know mad-at-the-world types who do actively try to be change agents but fall short because they can't get out of their own way.

In politics, there are some self-described advocates who equate activity with action, but those two things are not the same. These so-called advocates publicly protest and take selfies so they can get some "likes" on social media, but they fail to move the needle on the real issues. They feed off outrage rather than working to solve problems. Anytime I've interacted with these mad-at-the-world people I find myself wanting to escape their presence – and fast. It's easy to be a complainer and to grump around because things aren't the way you want them. It's more difficult to take action, drive change and get results through effective leadership.

Falling victim to the mad-at-the-world disorder is not constructive. Instead, we should channel our frustration and anger into leadership and transform the aspects of society that we simply cannot tolerate. This type of leadership, and the path to finding it, may look different depending on our perspectives, goals and strengths. But there are skills, tools, and nuances that are helpful no matter who we are or where we come from.

Before we can explore that toolbox laid out further in this book, we must first reflect on the type of leader we are and the type of leader we want to be. Only then can we determine our goals as well as who we want, or need, around us to achieve those objectives. But who we want around us and who we need around us may not always be one and the same. For example, I can think of times when I simply wanted someone there to affirm that I was making the right decisions and was on the best path possible. In truth, what I really needed was someone with a clear head to challenge the direction I was headed.

Getting clear on who we are is not as easy it sounds. Being honest with ourselves about our strengths and weaknesses in determining the type of leader we want to become is even more difficult. Politics is full of people without self-awareness. I've marveled at how many elected officials see themselves as charismatic visionaries when they were only elected because of a voter-turnout issue or because no one else wanted to run.

During one election cycle, I watched an ambitious, charming young man run for a statewide office. He had charisma on the campaign trail, and he recited talking points well. However, he had no leadership vision and was unable to translate those talking points into anything of substance. He was advised to take some time to learn about politics and governing behind the scenes, but he thought that was unnecessary. He turned down a job offer to work in a congressman's D.C. office because he thought he was ready to be in a leadership position; he didn't need to be anyone's understudy. Charm and ambition help on the campaign trail, but there needs to be some substance backing all that up. He didn't have it and voters could tell. He lost his race by a wide margin.

Knowing what type of leader you are helps determine how you can most effectively lead an organization or group of people. There are many different leadership styles and various methods in which individuals use their skills and abilities to get results. For example, some leaders are nurturers, while others are delegators. Some give regular feedback as a tool for managing relationships, while others use feedback sparingly. I've watched some elected officials who could rally people around most any issue with ease, and others who were much more effective legislating behind the scenes. I've also seen some leaders of Fortune 500 companies who were excellent at expanding their organization's footprint when the business climate was strong, but struggled managing crises when they inevitably crept up. This taught me that some leaders excel at growing organizations while others are better at managing through tough times and economic circumstances. One leadership style isn't necessarily better than any other, but the leader must be aware of how he or she uses each style to get results.

I worked with a Missouri state representative who was a fantastic public speaker. She could carry a room and make her point as eloquently as anyone I had ever seen. She was particularly passionate about reproductive choice. However, I noticed once when an abortion bill was being debated on the floor that she never spoke about how the legislation was harmful to women. When I asked her about it, she told me she knew herself well enough to know that her passion could be a double-edged sword. She didn't speak about the bill during the public debate because she was concerned that same passion on the subject would complicate her ability to do something about this potentially harmful legislation. She also knew other legislators didn't possess her negotiating skills but were effective speakers. By understanding her own leadership strengths, she positioned herself to be the lead negotiator behind the scenes and reserved her oratory skills for a rally with advocates later that evening.

Most of us recognize that there are areas where we need to grow to be more effective leaders. As I've said, I am not patient at all. My lack of patience can be helpful when I must push for quick results on multiple fronts. However, being impatient is not always a virtue when it comes to moving public opinion. A good example of that was an April 2019 ballot initiative that would have expanded quality Pre-K programs to more Kansas City families with four-year-olds. Education is one issue that lights my fire because I know firsthand how access to education can change an individual's forward momentum. The Mayor's Education Advisor led a lengthy study over several years examining Pre-K systems in other cities. She also engaged local parents and educators so we would understand the existing barriers to Pre-K. We were convinced that expanding Pre-K was an essential requirement for combatting everything from economic inequality to violent crime.

However, timing is everything at the ballot box and we had two big problems. The first was that this was our eighteenth election and most of the other campaigns raised taxes to address the problem at hand. Because Missouri residents are taxed at a relatively low rate, Kansas City receives a small amount of state funding for basic services compared to our peer cities in other states. In order to implement critical projects such as our streetcar system, $800 million worth of deferred infrastructure needs, or providing healthcare to the city's most vulnerable populations, we had to either renew a tax or create one for Kansas City – and this required the electorate to vote. During Sly's last few months in office, we proposed a new three-eighths of a cent sales tax increase to fund Kansas City's first citywide Pre-K program. Surely, I thought, voters will see that education of four-year-old children is worth three-eighths of a cent.

Our second problem with this effort was the fact that our city was behind the curve in viewing Pre-K as critical step in a child's development. Other cities had to take Pre-K initiatives to the ballot box two or three times before they passed, so this wasn't unusual. Unfortunately, with the end of Sly's mayoral term nearing, time was not on our side.

Kansas City voters had developed tax-increase fatigue. As the farmers back in North Carolina would say, "You can only go to the well so many times before it runs dry." We also didn't have enough time or campaign funding to educate voters about the short-term and long-term benefits of Pre-K. The education industry – from the school districts to the teachers' union -- certainly didn't help matters when they engaged in a turf war over how the funds would be distributed to families. In their view, the plan was flawed if they didn't control the funding. End of story.

I wish I had more patience with the whole process. Maybe we should have embarked on an intensive public-awareness campaign just to elevate the issue of quality Pre-K. Then later we could have asked voters to approve a new program. Sometimes the public needs to take baby steps toward fully embracing a public policy issue. At the time, we felt constrained by term limits and the need to solve the problem of too few children in quality Pre-K programs. In the moment, not pushing the idea in a big way seemed a waste of time, but I've often wondered if exercising more patience would have been the better route to go. Values-based leadership means you meet people where they are, even if they aren't where you want them to be. Values-based leadership theories suggest that leaders immerse themselves in understanding why people, or groups of people, feel the way they do. This is easier said than done sometimes, particularly when time isn't on your side, and there are four-year-olds who need help with both academic and socio-emotional skills so that they start kindergarten ready to learn.

As we think about understanding our leadership qualities, use these steps as a guide to taking action, driving change and getting results:

- Get a handle on the type of leader you are.
- Determine what exactly you want to see as a result of your leadership.
- Consider ways you want to build your leadership skill set.

Having clear goals in mind has often helped me assess how well I've managed my own time in addition to how well I've employed the efforts and skills of those around me. Knowing what you want to accomplish at the start of any project or program allows you to more easily reflect on the process you took to achieve your goals after you've reached them.

I was introduced to a woman who felt very strongly about women's health and specifically, reproductive rights. At the time we met, she was planning to run for City Council. The role any City Council plays in reproductive choice is minimal compared to state and federal government. After we mapped out her short- and long-term goals, she realized that she was only considering running for City Council because the seat happened to be available, and she perceived her chances of winning as better than average. However, that role wouldn't have given her the platform she needed to influence the issue she cared most about. Getting clear about her leadership goals showed her a more direct path to making the difference she wanted.

When it comes to accomplishing goals and leading people or organizations, I see individuals falling into one of two categories: process-oriented or results-oriented.

People who are more process-oriented highly value the road traveled to achieve results. They tend to focus on stakeholder engagement, broad values, and milestones. Those who fall into the results-oriented category are less focused on how the task at hand is accomplished and more geared toward getting the job done, so the next task can be tackled. Both types of skillsets are important and useful. The trick is to seamlessly combine them, and that takes knowing where both types of people can best use their skills.

I'm more of a results-oriented individual. However, at one time the Mayor's office staff that I led included a majority of process-oriented individuals. These staff members paid close attention to detail, and when it came to engaging diverse groups of stakeholders, they exercised an amount of patience that I could never summon. They also excelled at tracking milestones and building relationships. But trouble arose when we found ourselves balancing multiple hot-button issues at once. Our office usually had a to-do list that was a mile long, and we had to act fast in order to keep up with the constant demands. There wasn't always time to "process things to death," as I sometimes heard myself say. My impatience could really show when I felt like the people around me were spending too much time in the minutiae and not enough time getting things done. It was also during these moments when I'm certain I came off as more of a bitch than a cupcake.

The staff and I had to learn how to use our unique strengths to get results. It was important to be honest with ourselves about where each of us could fit into a solution and the Mayor's agenda. I was not the best person to serve on a long-term board or commission. Those assignments were a better fit for someone with more patience and with process-oriented skills. I was a better fit for handling things like crisis communications and political negotiations. Those situations fit my strong desire to get results and move onto the next highly charged issue – of which there were plenty!

Throughout my career and depending on the issue, I've sought guidance and insights from everyone from my grandparents to high-ranking government officials. Everyone needs a tribe from time to time. A tribe is a support network and can include mentors, sponsors, or people who have known you since you were a kid. Some people refer to this group as their "personal Board of Directors." Whether you're working through a personal issue, leading a government body or a large corporation, you need your tribe. Hopefully, you're stocking your tribe with people who support and challenge you.

I can always count on Mindy Mazur and Amy Jordan Wooden, two people in my tribe, to tell me exactly what I need to hear, even when I don't want to hear it. I dubbed them the "truth-sayers" for a reason. I have no doubts that they've saved me from several missteps through the years. Everyone needs at least one person in their life like this.

Mindy and Amy corrected me when I was absolutely convinced that I was handling a staffing situation well. Both women also prompted me to consider that just because I felt strongly about an issue didn't mean that everyone else did, or that the time was right to push it. They were also were quick to remind me that it is actually a journalist's job to write both sides of a story and not just the one I wanted them to write. Thankfully, this prevented me from sending emails I had already written to a couple of reporters. At least it was cathartic to write out my feelings in the heat of the moment. Had I not listened to my tribe though, my already rocky relationship with one certain member of the press could have taken a turn for the worse.

Cindy Circo was Kansas City's Mayor Pro Tem from 2011-2015 and another valued member of my tribe. Cindy's family has a long history of political involvement. We met shortly after I moved to Kansas City in 2011 and I began working in the Mayor's Office. Cindy is not one to give up on any issue easily. So, if she suggests that I leave an issue or project alone, then I listen. That type of guidance is crucial for an impatient, results-driven person like me. I trust her judgment because I've seen her tenacity in action.

She also knows the risk of taking things too far, whether it be in a political negotiation or building a business.

I had the opportunity to work closely with Cindy in 2014 when she was leading an effort to create what became Swope Soccer Village, a world-class soccer park in the city's urban core. Cindy worked to add to the vibrancy of the neighborhood and ensure the children in Kansas City's urban core had the same amenities and access to soccer as their peers in the wealthier suburbs. She also saw Swope Soccer Village as an economic plus to the neighborhood.

Few public policy issues are as convoluted as economic development. On the one hand, developers and their attorneys frequently do themselves a disservice by communicating poorly with the public about their deals. And on the other hand, government is not always stellar about educating the public on how economic development tools and processes work. In the end, these two factors tend to create discontent within communities. Misinformation, and a few people with mad-at-the-world disorder, lead to a community distrustful of economic development opportunities. Add to that, the media often fuels the fire between those two sides to create a juicy story.

In the case of Swope Soccer Village, Cindy was not a person to shrink in the face of conflict, particularly when she was working to better her community. Partial funding for this soccer park came from an economic development tool called Tax Increment Financing, or TIF. Through TIF, developers and governmental bodies enter into agreements on properties that often have been vacant, abandoned or dilapidated for years. These properties have been generating very little tax revenue for any government entity, including cities, counties, and local school districts. A TIF agreement allows a portion of future tax revenues re-invested into the project, enabling developers to capture the necessary revenues for rehabilitating the property. In other words, the developer puts in the money up front and is reimbursed for allowable expenses through some of the future tax revenue for the developed property. This reduces the developer's risk, which spurs economic development. Contrary to popular belief, TIF agreements do not set up a scenario where developers dip into current coffers of any governmental body's budget.

The area's school district sued the city over the development because they didn't want the funding from their portion of the TIF to be used for the soccer complex. Because Cindy was leading this effort for the City, she faced public scrutiny from the mad-at-the-world contingency who made no effort to understand the true positive impacts of the deal. She had to defend the complex's funding in court and in the media for months.

Once the funding for the soccer complex was finally in place, another hiccup arose when a local youth soccer club complained that Swope Soccer Village might create logistical issues for them. Comments they made during public hearings and to the media made it clear that they were also concerned that the complex would create new competition for them. Members demanded unreasonable access to the complex and dramatically reduced fees for their soccer club to use the facility. This would have placed the financial viability of the project at risk. Cindy and I worked together on this stage of the negotiations for weeks. At the time, I had a brand-new baby girl at home and had just returned to work from maternity leave. It was an inspiring time for me to sit at a decision-making table with a strong female leader who was not intimidated by anything. It was also comforting when she would shoo me out the door when our meetings had dragged into the evening. She didn't want me missing precious time with my baby if I didn't have to. Cindy raised two boys and understood the difficulty of being fully present at work when your heart is with your child, particularly in those early days.

Before a negotiating session, one of the men who led the negotiation efforts for the local soccer club walked into the conference room for our meeting and completely changed his posture when he realized two women would be negotiating on the city's behalf. It was clear he thought he could walk all over us.

During the negotiations, Cindy showcased her aptitude for getting things done by having a clear vision of what she wanted to accomplish and knowing at what point compromise was off the table. For example, she let the local soccer club know immediately that the sweetheart deal they wanted would jeopardize the financial health of the complex and she would not allow that to happen. Furthermore, her mastery of the intricate details of the project – everything from engineering to the financial forecast – blew me away. It was striking to me that her knowledge of the project was much more sophisticated than that of the men in the room who were negotiating against us. Working with her on Swope Soccer Village taught me the value of preparation and patience – skills I continue to work on as a results-oriented leader. The other side would have pounced if Cindy walked into the negotiations unprepared and timid. Instead, she knew her stuff, came off as confident and in control, and would not let anything stand in the way of her goal.

Everyone needs someone in their tribe who fully believes they can do anything. A few of us even get to count our spouse as that person. My husband, Fred, is wickedly smart in addition to being warm and gentle in all the ways I am not. But what initially attracted me to him was his positive outlook on everything. Where some people see problems and complaints, he sees opportunities and promise. This positive outlook is also linked to his unwavering confidence in me. I have never encountered a problem, personally or professionally, that he didn't believe I could conquer.

When Sly and I started thinking about launching our consulting firm, I was a bit hesitant about Fred's reaction. There were certainly positives and negatives with taking this leap into entrepreneurship. Being my own boss would mean I would have greater control over my schedule, something I had never experienced after nearly twenty years working in politics where long hours and stress are the norm year around. As Chief of Staff to a big city mayor, there were definitely times when my family got the short end of the stick. Managing the consequences of a major crime or winter storm on a large city doesn't usually happen only within the confines of regular business hours. Since Fred is a self-employed labor attorney, if I started my own business that would mean our entire household income would be unpredictable. We would have to figure out health insurance after enjoying the city's relatively inexpensive and robust health insurance plan. Considering the cash flow issues of most start-ups, we would also have to figure out how to manage retirement savings as well as saving for our daughter's college education without a consistent income. That's a lot to ask of any spouse.

Thankfully, he has always been supportive and steps up at home whenever client work takes me out of town or leaves me getting home late at night. He's said many times since we've been together that if he were going to start a new business then he'd want me to join him because he believes in my abilities and vision. I couldn't ask for a better member of my tribe.

When I speak to young women about career choices and leadership, I always tell them that they shouldn't feel like they have to be in an interpersonal relationship or domestic partnership. However, if they find themselves with a long-term partner, then it's important to choose wisely, and for the two of them to share values and goals. This includes issues like how housework or parenting is divided; every conceivable detail should be discussed. No one person can do everything for the family. Partnerships must be based on the equal distribution of everything and the trust and understanding that "equal" sometimes means 90 percent to 10 percent when professional obligations require it. And vice versa. I know when I'm under a tight deadline at work that Fred will pick up the slack at home, and I will do the same for him.

I've seen Fred whip up a waffle for our daughter quicker than I can. He's not afraid of the carpool line at school and he knows his way around a pediatrician's office, too. He's still working on learning how a leotard should fit a first grader, but no one is perfect all the time. In addition to a thriving law practice, Fred is also a singer-songwriter. This role means he spends time on some weekends and evenings rehearsing, performing and recording new material. During these times, I pick up the slack like he does for me.

My ability to function and thrive in my career would have been much different – particularly while serving as Chief of Staff and on-call all day, every day – if our relationship wasn't built on equality and agreeing to the terms before we married.

I also find that a balance between home and work is a difficult thing to strike within the constructs of today's family and work environment. Whenever I've focused on finding "balance" I have found myself to be more stressed and less pleasant to be around. Rather, I try to be more present in each moment. If I'm working on a project with a client, then I'm all in. If I'm swimming with my daughter at the YMCA, then I block out the thought of emails piling up in my inbox. Certainly, a strong tribe can help reinforce healthy habits, like self-care and being present. Your tribe can also help you define what success should look like for you as well as setting realistic expectations.

Understanding the types of people you need around you requires self-awareness and reflection. An additional layer of your self-awareness and reflection also calls for recognizing the usefulness and importance of incorporating diverse perspectives into your network. Your network should be diverse and include people who represent different demographics – race, sexual orientation, religion, gender – than you. I've found that this increases your leadership ability because it gives you a basic understanding of how different people or groups think, and how their value system is influenced. It's much more difficult to lead people when you are not able to understand where they're coming from or what's important to them.

I've frequently been admonished by Democratic friends for having close friends who are members of the Republican party. I find this hyper-partisan approach to people and situations to be odd. We should all be capable of maintaining our own political identity without administering some sort of political purity test before striking up a friendship with anyone. Having relationships with people who are Republican has made me better at my job. Thanks to those relationships, I have some context for Republican-leaning perspectives on political issues and am better able to see areas of compromise. I think life could get boring if you only surround yourself with people who think the same way you do and have similar life experiences.

Similarly, some women view all men as the enemy. This outlook seems self-defeating to me. The more we bring men into the conversation about women's leadership the better off women will be. I've seen how important supportive men can be to women leaders. I don't subscribe to the viewpoint that "women leaders don't need the help of a man." If a man is willing to use his power and platform to support and elevate women leaders, then we should encourage him to do exactly that. Leveraging the power men have in society is not the same as being dependent on them.

Leaders should be collaborative, but not dependent. And leaders must recognize that regardless of where you lead – elected office, the board room, or something different – HOW you lead is important. Leadership is not about perfection – it's about honing your skills so that you can take action, drive change and get results.

Being perpetually dissatisfied and mad-at-the-world doesn't accomplish your goals. Another piece of wisdom Grandpa Chamblee dished out was, "if you're not willing to help make something right, then stop complaining about it being wrong." Complaining is not leadership. Leaders get things done, move the needle and make their organization or community better.

Chapter 5
Failing Up

We all know that one person who tends to be in the room whenever there's a significant meeting or a policy discussion. This person's influence is marginal, but he – or she – has a seat at the table. How does that happen? This person's knowledge on the subject matter is inconsequential, but the perception is that he or she has something to contribute so they're there. We often wonder what they bring to the conversation.

Leadership should not be confused with just finding a way to be in the room when decisions are made. Many of us have probably had experiences with people who are considered "leaders" in some groups without the bona fides to go along with such a characterization. Despite lacking results, they rise through the ranks and exemplify the term "failing up." I worked with one man who managed to climb the ladder without honing any discernible skill set other than having a pleasant demeanor and a well-connected family. Of course, it helps to be friendly to people. And good for him that he practically came out of the womb with a strong network of influential civic leaders at his disposal.

But through the years, he fumbled his way through high-profile political issues, flaked out on his team when a situation was more difficult than he anticipated, and screwed up relationships because of his failure to see a project through until the end. Yet, there he was in countless rooms with influential people.

He was adept at using social media to highlight and celebrate his so-called achievements. He appeared to have a reputation as a rising leader in the community. But he was "failing up" because he was born on third base with all the privilege that means. He was in the room, but he wasn't a leader.

"Failing up" is easier for individuals of privilege – male or female. In my experience, the more privilege you have, the less likely you are to face bias in the workplace and in society. When privileged individuals do face bias, they often have an easier time overcoming it. I supervised a college intern whose work product and work ethic were mediocre, but he still managed to land a White House internship the next semester. His mother was well-connected in business and political circles and, to her credit, was committed to exposing him to a variety of experiences. Another intern, a black female, consistently performed well throughout her internship and always asked for additional responsibilities. She excelled at school and worked a part-time job to help with the family's expenses. Her tenacity was indispensable to her success. Without a doubt, her mom was as dedicated to her personal and professional growth as the young man's mother, but this mother lacked the privilege and connections to get her daughter into the White House.

I think of those two interns often and their very different frames of reference. I can't help but assume that the young man will continue to "fail up" in his career. Yet, the young woman will probably have to continue to fight her way to get where she belongs, her margin for error always being smaller than his.

The reality is, for those of us from modest backgrounds, there is usually little room for error. It is important to understand, however, that we each bring a unique set of attributes and experiences to the table. Here's an example: Early on, I wasn't exposed to many traditional experiences, like museum trips and vacations, that middle class children typically have. However, the experiences I did have still taught me important lessons about honesty, resiliency, and how to communicate with people of diverse backgrounds. You don't necessarily need money to learn important life lessons. But it is helpful for you, as a leader, to consider how privilege contributes to "failing up," and how you can address it.

Organizational leaders can help set standards for what qualifies as expertise and success by identifying performance measures and goals for each staff member. Not only does this help establish expectations for both staff and supervisors, but it also makes it more difficult to "fail up" if the work product is consistently measured. Consistent feedback loops between staff members and their supervisors can also help everyone better understand any cultural or institutional roadblocks that might hinder an individual's ability to succeed. Understanding and dismantling those roadblocks is a necessary and complementary step for organizations to make it more difficult for individuals to "fail up." These two steps are not the same thing, but both are necessary.

It's important to think about gender dynamics, specifically gender bias, when we're looking at how and why some people "fail up." Tomas Chamorro-Premuzic posed an interesting question in an article he published in January of 2020 posing an interesting question – "Why Do So Many Incompetent Men Become Leaders and What Can We Do About It?" His thesis is that "men are typically more deceived about their talents than women are. And they are also more likely to succeed in their careers." He encourages us to consider not only why "there aren't any more women leaders, but why do so many incompetent men become leaders?" His research suggests that the answer is threefold: 1) We are not deft at deciphering between confidence and competence; 2) We're naturally drawn to charismatic individuals; and 3) Consciously or not, we are attracted to narcissists.

I agree with Chamorro-Premuzic's findings. But I also believe that many organizations fail to adequately address the systemic issue of incompetent men – who have an overinflated view of their skills – becoming leaders. Automatic male promotion perpetuates gender bias. If women are to overcome this bias, we must share stories of how we've dealt with challenging situations involving misplaced achievement. Unless we share our stories, the knowledge we have gained helps no one else.

It's important to include men in the process of dismantling bias. When men use their voice and their influence to object to other men "failing up," we can more quickly dismantle the norms, barriers, and biases that prevent women from taking leadership positions that they're often better suited for than the men who occupy them. Finally, we must build women's confidence by overcoming impostor syndrome, which we'll discuss in detail in Chapter Seven. When women know they have the right to be in the room, at the table, and making decisions, then they're more likely to recognize "failing up" when it's in front of them.

We should all worry about our society's perception of leadership in this age of social media impressions, broadcast soundbites, and incessant digital connection. Social media makes it easier to put forward an image of "success" without having actually accomplished much. Someone who is social media savvy can use it to "fail up." Political candidates are certainly guilty of using social media to convey false achievement or acceptance, but the boardroom has its own brand of "smoke and mirrors," like confusing activity with action. Have you ever seen a colleague who is always "busy" with meetings, but those meetings never translate into measurable results? It's not unlike elected officials who spend more time on Twitter than balancing budgets or solving constituents' problems.

Leadership shouldn't be measured in anything remotely resembling "likes" and retweets. When hiring for staff positions in government and on campaigns, I tried to determine whether the individual had any real idea of what they would be getting into. Did they understand the workload and its expectations? I interviewed a few potential staff members and it was clear to me that they were more interested in moving their career along than doing the arduous, sometimes unglamorous, work of campaigns or public service. When I asked one interviewee to tell me the biggest opportunity she saw in the position if she was hired, her response was, "My Twitter feed!" She wasn't joking. She went on to tell me how excited she was about the exposure the position could bring to her. Her lack of understanding about public service was as disappointing as it was troubling. Needless to say, she didn't get the job, but she's still a frequent flyer on Twitter.

My career in public service was more than a career; it was a lifestyle. The long hours required means your life is not your own. There were countless times over the years where I'd find myself on a conference call late at night or during the weekend. Campaigns, in particular, are a 24/7 endeavor.

The pay is typically not stellar in public service. During the last couple of years that I was the Mayor's Chief of Staff, I decided against taking any sort of raise. Because of the classification of my job, we would have had to get an ordinance passed through the City Council for my salary to increase even a nickel. I expected any ordinance our office wanted, particularly one that would have increased my salary, would have become a political lightning rod. Rather than put the Mayor, and myself, through that I kept my salary stagnant.

Selflessness is another job requirement. Public service is about serving the public and not about serving yourself. Over the years, I saw some political staffers struggle to understand this and to live it as a philosophy every day. A couple of staffers in the Missouri State Capitol were infamous for going from office to office asking for tickets to sporting events and concerts. This seemed so tacky. It was hard for me to imagine their reputation as moochers didn't affect their ability to do their jobs. Unfortunately, in today's political and corporate worlds where the tendency is towards self-aggrandizement and self-promotion, we sometimes see less leadership and more showmanship.

Top Ten Leadership Lessons

Public service taught many leadership lessons that I learned on-the-job and are applicable to other sectors as well. Here are my Top Ten Leadership Lessons:

Lesson One: Resiliency is your body armor.

Regardless of your leadership position or the sector you're working in, it's inevitable that things will sometimes go wrong. The key is to get up when you fall and try again. The good news is resiliency can be built. Think of it like building a suit of armor. Maybe you start with a shield and then add a helmet. You keep building that protective layer until you're completely fortified.

One place to start when fashioning your armor is the Marine Corps' unofficial slogan: "Improvise, Adapt, and Overcome." Moviegoers may have first heard it in Clint Eastwood's *Heartbreak Ridge*. Sly was a Marine, so he infused this slogan into our daily lives in the Mayor's Office. Remembering this slogan certainly helped reframe our minds when we found ourselves in difficult situations. Our "resiliency armor" improved when we began to believe that a crisis was not insurmountable. Remember that some of the best ideas occur when things don't go as planned. Even one of the most common office supplies, the Post-it Note, was created by mistake. Keep things in perspective.

It's also important to focus on the positive. If you stay in a negative mindset then you can expect negative results. A positive outlook is another piece of body armor in your resiliency suit. And keeping a positive outlook also includes nurturing a positive view of yourself. This is where resisting the urge to compare yourself to others is instrumental, as is establishing realistic goals for yourself. Goals are not constructive if they set you up for failure. At the same time, don't be afraid to establish goals that push you to grow. This is a balance that isn't always easy to strike, but when done well, can help you manage your own emotions and expectations of the people around you. Give these tips to your colleagues and staff as they may need your help to improve their resiliency.

After working with some staff members who tended to crumble at the first sign of trouble, I began incorporating questions in the hiring process to determine the interviewee's ability to bounce back. I would prod them to respond to questions about how they would reframe expectations when it was obvious an initial goal wasn't feasible. Or I'd ask how they react to criticism. I would even ask them to give me an example of when they were resilient in a previous role. I found that it's easier to teach someone how a bill becomes a law than to teach someone to be resilient.

As if running a major city wasn't enough, the Sly James administration also ran eighteen elections over the course of eight years in the Mayor's Office. Missouri's State Constitution required a public vote to increase taxes, and if we were going to achieve many of our goals that involved rebuilding crumbling infrastructure and investing in public transit, then we had to find the funding to do it. That meant convincing voters to increase their taxes. Our track record still boggles my mind – we won sixteen of those eighteen elections. We wanted to use every moment we had in office wisely and that meant we rarely sat still. We needed to have mental toughness and resiliency to keep up this pace.

As the Chief of Staff I had the opportunity to meet resilient people that otherwise I would probably never have had the chance to meet. One of them was Rosilyn Temple. Violent crime was a major focus for our mayoral administration. I met Rosilyn through that work and quickly saw her mental toughness and resiliency was her armor built from unspeakable grief. She lost her son in 2011 to gun violence. No one would blame her if she remained consumed by her sorrow. But that's not who Rosilyn is. She formed the Kansas City chapter of Mothers in Charge, whose mission is to reduce violent crime through prevention, education, and intervention, as well as supporting victims' families. She built the trust of the community and the local law enforcement officials and is an important player in efforts to reduce crime in Kansas City.

Being resilient also might earn you a new nickname. The Dover Group, a political and public affairs consulting firm, played a critical role in electing Sly to his first term as mayor in 2011 and in each of the seventeen campaigns thereafter. In early 2018, Mark Nevins of the Dover Group and I were discussing a variety of political issues that the Mayor's office was currently facing when he gave me a nickname about my ability to be resilient. He called me "Ex-Lax." Mark considered this name appropriate because I tend to "Make shit happen." I've always thought it was fitting!

Lesson Two: Conflict isn't necessarily bad.

Conflict may arise when there are differing opinions on an issue. Public service taught me that conflict is often a necessary part of social and organizational change. Thinking of all conflict as inherently bad misses an important point: managing conflict is an opportunity to make positive change and to bridge differing viewpoints. That's a good thing.

Leaders, whether in government or the private sector, increasingly rely on data and research to inform their decision-making. This can be a scary paradigm shift for some, especially employees of those organizations. Employees may initially be concerned that the data will reveal that their work isn't producing the results managers want to see and therefore, result in negative consequences. Managers may then implement different strategies and techniques to improve results. Conflict often occurs in situations like this because the unknowns and newness of change can be scary for employees.

Effective leaders manage through this type of conflict by clearly communicating the value of using data to make decisions and new strategies to improve performance. They also celebrate successes, particularly the successes of employees, and are careful to continuously educate them on the usefulness of tracking data. It can be easy at the first sign of conflict with a paradigm shift like this, to resort back to the status quo – but that's not leadership, it's preservation. Preservationists, in this sense, balk when they experience push back. Leaders find ways to connect people with their vision.

We'll discuss more about leading through conflict and specific issues women face when navigating conflict in Chapter 11, *Navigating Conflict While Female.*

Lessons Three and Four: Talk less. Listen more.

Talk less and listen more – it's particularly true if you're a white dude. Now, more than ever, we see how important it is to listen diverse viewpoints.

Active listening is a critical communication skill that is often overlooked. Your listening skills – or the lack thereof – are foundational for how you can lead to take action, drive change and get results. And for results-driven people like me who can be impatient, active listening can help us check ourselves. Active listening is paying focused attention, deferring judgment and providing feedback. This skill helps us open and broaden our perspective to what the other person is actually saying versus what we want them to say. It's easy to hear someone's words and say, "Aha! I know what she means by that!" when we're in a hurry to wrap up a project. However, active listening requires you to stop and pay attention to the speaker, not make rash judgements and provide appropriate feedback.

Good listening skills also help widen our worldview. I've been grateful when I've come to the table with an open mind. I have sometimes realized I had formed my own assumptions and was looking at an issue through a biased lens. Active listening lessens the chance that you'll fall victim to such biases. Whether you're in the board room, in Congress, or leading your neighborhood association, it's important to check yourself (and ask your tribe for feedback) on your listening skills. Our government, and many companies, would function better if more people listened *to* each other rather than talked *at* each other.

I cherish the friendships I made with the talented individuals at Kit Bond Strategies (KBS), a consulting firm focusing on business development and government relations. The KBS team represented the City of Kansas City in Washington, D.C. They advocated for our public policy agenda, which included increasing funding for transportation, accomplishing our housing priorities, and connecting us with programs that would help our city address gun violence and educational inequities.

I had weekly conference calls with KBS colleagues: Shana Marchio, Matt Roney and Mitch Erdel to discuss city issues. We'd also catch up on our families, our problems, and successes. Matt said several times that listening to Shana and I tell our stories about that thin line between Cupcake and Bitch made him look at things in ways he hadn't before. He widened his viewpoint about women's experiences in the workplace because he genuinely listened to us.

My relationship with that team increased my own understanding of how the "other side of the aisle" looks at public policy and political issues. Each of us had our own perspectives on everything from reproductive choice to taxes and we were open to listening to the other's opinion – not just hearing it. We didn't necessarily change our positions on issues, but we did better understand where the other side was coming from. On more than one occasion, a conversation with the KBS team helped me understand the opposing viewpoint.

Lesson Five: Compromise isn't a dirty word; it's how things get done.

Too often in our modern political environment, compromise is considered a sign of weakness. Through the years, I've seen factions on both sides of the aisle whine when Republicans and Democrats do manage to come together and forge consensus on an issue. Some people just feed off hate and discontent. They'd rather see political infighting than compromise and solutions. This is destructive to political discourse and our democracy.

The City's budget process was also an annual exercise in compromise. Kansas City's charter required the Mayor and City Council to pass a balanced budget each year – no printing money at City Hall! Before the vote on the budget, the Mayor's Office is inundated with budget requests. More often than not, the requests are for programs and initiatives worthy of funding. However, there is only so much city funding to go around. Compromise truly is the engine of this process. Interest groups rarely got all the funding they wanted, but we tried to help organizations capture private and philanthropic funding where possible to make tax dollars go further.

When working on a compromise for an issue, whether you're involved in a political negotiation or a business deal, it's important to focus on ideas and not people. Since your foe on one issue may be your staunchest ally on the next, you need to concentrate on combatting the details of the issue that need changing. We are all human and, therefore, challenged by emotions from time to time. But we must do our best to remain focused on finding the compromise rather than on personalities. Emotions like revenge and self-interest are not only damaging to compromise, but also to careers.

Many progressive advocates opposed our Pre-K ballot measure because, in their view, it was a regressive tax and would disproportionately hurt poor Kansas Citians. I was frustrated that I couldn't get them to see that no other funding stream was available, and that the Pre-K initiative would help poor families access quality, affordable Pre-K programs. I tried to separate our political disagreements from our friendships; sometimes I was even successful at doing so. Several of the most outspoken opponents of the Pre-K initiative are proponents of policy issues that I believe are extremely important, like Medicaid expansion and gun control. So, we may not align on every issue, but there are certainly some where we can lock arms.

Lesson Six: Know a crisis when you see it.

Not everything is a crisis. If you treat everything like it is, then you're going to have a tough time regardless of what role you play in your organization or community. Kindergarteners at my daughter's elementary school learn the differences between a glitch, a bummer and a disaster – lessons in resiliency can start early! As an adult, I ask myself when faced with some sort of drama: Is this an issue, a problem, or a crisis? Those three things are not the same.

I once supervised a young man who was constantly in a state of panic about something. Every single thing he was involved in was a crisis to him. This showed me he lacked self-awareness and situational awareness, and above all, he wasn't ready to be a leader. Every situation is different, but consider these three questions when you think you may be navigating a crisis:

- Is someone's safety at risk?
- Is an individual's or organization's reputation at risk?
- Is the mission of the organization or individual in jeopardy?

If the answer is "no" to these three questions, then you should not treat the situation as a crisis. If you answer "yes" to at least one, your situation is likely still not a crisis, but rather an issue or a problem.

My friend and colleague, Roy Temple, was the Chief of Staff for Governor Mel Carnahan and later Senator Jean Carnahan. During one of my regular chats with Roy, I vented about a contentious issue I was dealing with in the Mayor's Office. In typical Roy fashion, he leaned back in his chair and told me that Chiefs of Staff get thrown the biggest problems facing the administration because if the problem was an easy one, then someone else would have already solved it. We talked through a few strategies he used to not only manage problems, but also his own emotions during tough times. This struck a chord with me and emphasized that not every issue should be considered a crisis. Roy reminded me that others on the staff would be looking to me to guide them, not just through the logistics of finding the needed solution, but emotionally as well. If I conveyed a sense of alarm, it would be a distraction. Something to remember – for better or worse – the leader sets the tone.

Lesson Seven: Your brand takes a long time to build and a short time to destroy.

Your personal brand is you. Similar to how a product interacts with the marketplace, your personal brand is how you interact with the public and is a combination of your reputation, style, and charisma. The foundational strategy in protecting your personal brand is to be honest in your interactions with others. Your personal and professional relationships will be stronger if you tell people the truth, no matter how difficult it is. Relationships are the foundation for being able to get things done. Dishonesty poisons relationships and your ability to be an effective leader.

Social media can be a useful tool or your worst enemy when it comes to building and protecting your personal brand. I cannot believe the things some otherwise self-actualized individuals will say on social media. Employers can easily turn to the internet to see how prospective and current employees present themselves on social media as well as their connections in the community. Remember this when considering posting something a little bitchy on social media channels. Use your voice effectively without jeopardizing your brand.

During the last several years as Chief of Staff, I was honored to develop a great working relationship, and a friendship, with Pastor Ron Lindsay of the Concord Fortress of Hope Church in south Kansas City. One day we talked about reputations. He told me how his own value system related to his personal brand: "Know who you are, embrace where you came from, and focus on where you want to be. After that, all that is left is to orient your actions accordingly." Amen to that.

Lesson Eight: Surround yourself with people who push you to be better.

You can't go wrong with people in your life who have higher expectations for you than you sometimes have for yourself. Your mentors, sponsors and tribe believe in you and challenge you when you need it. Women, who are more likely to experience impostor syndrome, should make an effort to have someone in their corner who pushes them to be better.

Officer Dennis Coates led Sly's security detail during the last few years of our administration. He was typically very quiet and reserved – apropos for his position. But he let his guard down, at least a little bit, to a few of us. This can happen when you spend hours driving or in meetings with someone. There were days and weeks that I'd see more of Dennis than Fred or Vivian.

During one out-of-town trip, Dennis and I had a particularly introspective discussion about the meaning of life and how we spend our time on Earth. Dennis had an impeccable work ethic. In fact, we talked a lot about how both of us probably subscribed more to the philosophy of "living to work" rather than "working to live." We both were fortunate enough to love what we did for a living and didn't see it as work at all. We saw our careers as extensions of ourselves, our personal interests and our values. He said that his commitment to his work pushed him to be a better person. He said serving in the Kansas City Police Department exposed him to problems and people he otherwise would not have met, and he learned from them. I knew exactly what he meant.

At the end of June 2019, Sly and I went to Honolulu for his last meeting of the U.S. Conference of Mayors. Sly had been in the group's leadership for several years, so they asked him to give some remarks about leadership. We were usually exhausted at the end of these meetings, but this one took even more out of us. After the conference, Sly left and I stayed for a well-deserved vacation with Fred, Vivian, and my stepdaughter, Libby.

The next morning, I woke up earlier than usual. I have no idea why. I saw that I had missed three phone calls and a slew of texts from Sly. Dennis had suffered a massive heart attack. He was only 53 years old and in great physical shape. Dennis worked out religiously and ate well. But he died that day.

It's not lost on me how Dennis was intently focused on continuously improving himself as a professional and as a person. I wish I had spent more time talking to him about that and less time venting about Kansas City politics. But even in that realization, Dennis' example of how to live encourages me to be a better person.

Lesson Nine: Build relationships with people of different backgrounds.

If politics is your lens, then make friends in a different political party. It will make you think about issues in a more holistic way. It will also help you serve the public better.

Regardless of your industry, seek out people to learn from and build relationships with those who don't look like you or live like you. This means everything from race and sexuality to religion and physical ability. Think about how you can forge connections with people who will challenge your assumptions, improve your empathy, and help you look at issues more holistically.

Effective leaders understand that diversity strengthens us. No one person has all the context they need to solve problems. And none of us hold all the answers to every dilemma. Building a diverse network is not only the right thing to do, but it's also a necessary step in assembling the wide variety of perspectives you'll inevitably need to achieve results.

For example, there is a reason why patients have a medical "team." Rarely does one medical professional have the perspective or detailed knowledge he or she needs to address the totality of someone's medical condition. Depending on the patient's ailment, the medical team may include a primary care physician, a nurse, and a specialist like a surgeon or physical therapist. By evaluating and treating the patient from their individual expertise, medical team members give the patient the most effective treatment to recover.

Lesson Ten: Say "no" at least as often as you say "yes."

If you aren't taking care of yourself then you can't take care of anyone else. Saying no is important if the return on investment falls short, or if it could detract from your personal brand. Later in this book, we'll discuss the concept of "non-promotable" tasks, and how women are often negatively impacted by them.

Leaders must understand that you can't please everyone, even those who want our time for whatever altruistic reason. Admittedly, I've learned this the hard way.

People are either givers or takers. Most of us aren't somewhere in between, even if we want to. I am a giver to a fault. My top two strengths in the Gallup StrengthsFinder analysis are Responsibility and Achiever. This is a great asset 60 percent of the time. It's a real burden for the remaining 40 percent.

I'm learning that saying no is a strength and not a sign of weakness. Dennis was the first person I've known who died unexpectedly. There were no good-byes. That shook me because it showed me again how fragile life is. One day you can be climbing a mountain like Dennis and the next day you can have a massive heart attack. How you spend your time matters.

I try to focus my time on what I feel like are my most precious assets: my family, health, and business. Lucky for me this includes work on issues like women's leadership and increasing access to educational opportunities. We all have plenty of things we'd like to do, but there are only so many hours in a day. If something is not your priority, it belongs on a different list.

Learning to say no is an important part of leadership. If you can't say no when your friend calls and asks for you to speak to their group for free, then how are you going to say no when you're faced with a decision that could negatively impact your personal brand? Similarly, if you're not used to saying no, then how will you do it when you reach a leadership position and realize that you can't say yes to every interest group?

Leadership is not a static term or condition. It can look differently in different organizations at different times. However, successful leaders do try to continuously improve their teams and recognizing who "fails up" is a factor that cannot be ignored. Similarly, leaders who can get the people within their organization to focus less on showmanship and more on results will be better able to drive change and accomplish their goals.

My Top Ten Leadership Lessons are helpful guides in developing your own skills and helping the people around you grow theirs, too. The farmers I grew up around would say, "There is more than one ingredient to a successful crop." The same can be said about leadership.

Chapter 6
Social Norms Are the Real *Bitch*

*T*he **thin line** between Cupcake and Bitch often enters the equation when a woman considers saying "no" to a task. Some of us just can't help ourselves from saying "yes" to everything, even when our capacity is limited because our to-do list is full. When I worked for the Senator, I heard someone say, "If you want something to get done, then give it to a busy woman!" We "busy women" straddle the thin line when it comes to saying "no." It's one thing to learn to say "no" to family or friends. It's quite another to say "no" to a supervisor who asks you to do a non-promotable task yet again. Most people would likely define your refusal as insubordination. That's why I believe social norms, like expectations, assumptions about productivity and time, and perceptions of power are the real bitches in the workplace. It's also why some women may step to the bitch side of the line when they are faced with this gender inequity.

Social norms are built from generations of socially acceptable behavior. In some cases, both men and women participate in unfair, gendered behavior reinforcing the biased social norms against women that we should be deconstructing. I've identified three strategies men and women can use to recalibrate those norms into positive, unbiased outcomes: reframe expectations; re-examine the concepts of scheduling and productivity; and, shift perceptions.

Reframe Expectations

Several years ago, a male colleague and I were discussing the merits of an early voting bill with a statewide elected official. I prepped for this meeting for days and anticipated the push back I'd get from him. I had responses for each of his issues and felt that, at the very least, he would not stand in the way of our efforts. I must have made my points well with the elected official because he told me he thought I had a career ahead of me in politics. But then he disqualified the comment I thought was a compliment when he said, "You'd make a great political spouse. You would do really well at fundraising events!"

He didn't see me as a public policy professional, a political communicator, or as someone who might have political ambitions of my own. Rather, he relegated my value to being marriage material. Some political spouses do play a substantive role in politics and policy. However, I didn't think that was his point. And so, I replied curtly, "I don't need to marry a politician to contribute to our democracy."

The elected official's expectations of me were created by what he saw through his own gendered, old-fashioned lens. My comment may not have completely changed his perspective, but I would hope it made him think twice about it. I couldn't help but think he made such a sexist comment because he was unfamiliar with women in leadership positions and had the audacity to articulate his own bias. Men have been running governments for a very long time. There are really no prerequisites for men to serve – certainly not marriage.

As we walked back to the office, my colleague admitted to me that he didn't think a comment like that would ever be directed toward a man. Women still don't hold leadership positions in government at the same rate as men and, because of that, some people still don't see them as natural leaders. Political spouses? Yes. Elected officials in their own right? Not so much.

In early 2013, I was the Director of Public Affairs for Mayor Sly James and my responsibilities included communications. I was also in my second trimester. I planned to be on maternity leave for eight weeks after Vivian was born and tried to wrap up all the major communications projects on our plates before her due date so the communications team could focus on day-to-day tasks.

Part of this preparation included having one-on-one discussions with all the reporters who covered politics and City Hall to advise them of the plan while I was on leave. One interaction left me stunned. After I told a male reporter that I would be on maternity leave for eight weeks, he told me that I should rethink returning to work as the Director of Public Affairs. He thought my work product would never be the same. He believed the demands of having a baby at home would interfere and diminish my ability to be responsive to the media at all hours.

I couldn't believe what I was hearing. I could almost feel my blood pressure rising. I had heard about other women's experiences with this reporter's blatant sexism and disrespect, but now I was living it. My reaction to him was probably not the height of professionalism by most standards. I admit that I lost my cool and probably crossed the line into bitchy territory. I told him, with some colorful language, that people with his viewpoint had no business in today's workplace.

This experience also made me wonder if other women were treated so poorly when they told employers that they were pregnant. I am white, middle class and had my boss – a mayor! – in my corner, and I was being told that I should just stay home after having my baby. I could only imagine how other working mothers who didn't have my privilege, like women of color or mothers working for minimum wage, may be treated at their places of employment.

These examples illustrate the biases and low expectations of women in the workplace, but there are other prejudices based on socio-economic status, race, sexual orientation, religion – even the name of the college on your diploma or the lack of a diploma. If you've ever been on the receiving end of someone's low expectations, then you know it can shake your confidence and leave you fuming. It's difficult to remove your emotions from situations like this, but the more objective you can be, the more likely you can turn a bad experience into a teachable moment.

Low expectations can be a product of someone's biases, which are created by their frame of reference and the dynamics either surrounding them from childhood or through life experiences. The statewide elected official and the reporter in the above examples clearly viewed women in the workplace and in civic leadership through their male-centered frames of reference. Those factors influenced their perceptions of what is possible and appropriate. Put simply, they viewed my goals and abilities through the lens of what felt normal to them. The teachable moment came when I explained the situation from my perspective. Hopefully, they listened and incorporated an additional perspective into their frame of reference.

Both men and women should understand that using only our own frame of reference as the measure for formulating realistic expectations of others is shortsighted and unfair. We are better off proactively interacting with different types of people and learning about their life experiences. Had the elected official in the story above been better at surrounding himself with more women in elected office, he may not have insinuated that marriage was my only route to political longevity. Similarly, had the reporter reached out to any working moms in the newsroom to learn how they manage their time and priorities, he may have known that it was actually possible to have a career and children at the same time – even if that career involved working odd hours.

Another reason we may find ourselves dealing with low expectations is self-sabotage. Realizing that we can sometimes be our own worst enemy can be a hard pill to swallow, but it's not uncommon. For example, a friend at a financial services company grew frustrated when she was repeatedly passed over for promotions. Her supervisor was male and had been with the company for thirty years. She was convinced there was gender bias at play. When she finally got the courage to ask her supervisor why she was stuck in her current position, his response surprised her. He said the leadership team was skeptical of her abilities as a manager because she frequently told them in evaluations that she couldn't see herself managing other employees. Even though she was an expert in her field, her own words were undercutting her professional growth. She was the definition of self-sabotage. When her supervisor offered to pay for professional development so that she could hone those supervisory skills, she declined because she didn't want those responsibilities. Perhaps impostor syndrome was at play or maybe she didn't fully explain to the leadership team why she was hesitant to supervise others. Regardless, in the end, her goals and expectations were not aligned with the opportunities at the company, and it was that misalignment impeding the growth she was looking for. Had everyone involved communicated clearly, this situation could have been avoided.

There are certainly times when low expectations are simply generated out of malice. For a variety of reasons, you may be confronted with someone who is outwardly and unapologetically demeaning. In those times, make a plan for how you will reframe their expectations. How are you most comfortable dealing with their belittling behavior? Do you want to address it head-on with the offender and call out their bad behavior? Or would you rather ignore them to the greatest extent possible? In some situations, a combination of both may be the best recipe.

Re-examine the Concepts of Scheduling and Productivity

It's no secret that for generations, men conducted business on the golf course and over cocktails after 5 p.m. In those days, women generally stayed home and took care of the children. Time management was simply plugging meetings into time slots that were free, and it didn't matter what was happening at home. Men were not juggling daycare drop-off responsibilities and their children's after-school activities.

Now, more women are not only working outside the home, but they're making strides in obtaining leadership positions across the board. This is changing the parameters of when business gets done and how organizations expect their employees to allocate their time. Flexible work schedules and telecommuting are becoming more widely accepted. Part-time positions are another way women or men can maintain a professional track while integrating personal commitments. Additionally, more working-age adults now find themselves caring for older family members, which adds to the pressure on organizations to think creatively about when and how business gets done.

The issue of time management became a focal point in our mayoral administration in 2014 when we worked with the Women's Foundation in Kansas City and commissioned a study on women's participation in civic engagement. The study's purpose was to understand the barriers to women serving on municipal boards and commissions. For three months, Dr. Barbara Kerr, a researcher and professor at the University of Kansas, studied responses from online surveys and focus groups to analyze quantitative and qualitative data on women's propensity to serve in this leadership capacity. The results told us that, "Women wanted to be absolutely sure that time was spent efficiently; that meetings were conveniently scheduled; and that they would see results of their efforts for the time spent." This study specifically focused on civic engagement, but the results highlighted the often-overlooked importance of time management for women in a broader sense as well.

Take networking, for instance. Trade associations, industry groups and membership organizations host many networking events throughout the year. Many of them are scheduled for 7:30 a.m. or 5 p.m. to accommodate work schedules. Networking has so much value, particularly for those whose friends or family lack strong professional connections to help open doors. But networking events scheduled outside normal business hours can create logistical problems for working women. This is all the more reason for those planners to ensure participants' time is used effectively.

I attended an early morning networking event with a female executive from a telecommunications company. She made me laugh out loud when she chastised the event organizers for hosting a 7:30 a.m. networking event without an agenda or any defined take-aways for the participants. "I do not need to come downtown for another donut," she said. "I had to figure out school transportation for two kids, reschedule a staff meeting, and miss my mother's doctor appointment for this. Next time, use my time wisely or you won't get another chance."

It's also important to consider what meetings and events must take place during early morning time frames and after normal business hours. Without question, some situations necessitate long and nontraditional hours. Others simply don't.

A mentor who was the President and CEO of a national nonprofit once told me that her rule for accepting meetings and events after 5 p.m. was based on whether or not the subject matter involved a crisis or whether the organization's mission couldn't move forward without the meeting taking place at that specific time. She was caring for her father who was in the late stages of Alzheimer's disease. She could easily swing a 7:30 a.m. breakfast meeting, but she felt like she needed to be home with her father in the evenings as the disease affected his emotional well-being after dark. "Even though my father's health is not my employer's problem," she said, "my peace of mind affects my ability to do my job and that is their problem." Her self-awareness helped her see that she was not at her best if her mind was elsewhere, so she scheduled her day accordingly when feasible. If her organization needed her to attend an event or to lead an important evening meeting, then she did so. But she, and her Board of Directors, became more discerning about when those occasions were warranted. Both workplaces and employees benefit when this type of discernment is embraced.

Her experience taught me an important lesson about managing my own scheduling to improve productivity. As Chief of Staff, I was working many long hours – it was part of the job description. I would wake up early Monday through Friday to prep for the day and work until 6 p.m. After Vivian went to bed, I spent the time reading legislation, writing speeches, drafting staff performance reviews, and answering the incessant emails that piled up during the day. But I was still getting frequent requests for 5 p.m. happy hour meetings to discuss city business. At first, I said "yes" too many times. I didn't want to be viewed as anything less than committed to the job – probably overcompensating for my terse interaction with the reporter who told me I couldn't do my job after the baby was born.

But the next time I was asked to meet over drinks, I decided to try a different approach. I pivoted the meeting to take place over breakfast after I dropped off Vivian at daycare. I was following the wise advice of Amy Jordan Wooden. "People want to meet with you because you're the Chief of Staff to the Mayor," she told me. "They aren't going to say 'no' to a meeting just because it takes place at 8:30 a.m. rather than 5:30 p.m. Make your position work for you." This allowed me the opportunity to start my day embracing the role of mom before transitioning into my role as Chief of Staff. I found a way to integrate both roles into my day rather than feeling like I had to pick one or the other.

Our views about work and family are shifting. Socially acceptable ideas about productivity and scheduling should change, too. Men and women in leadership should push forward a new paradigm for integrating work and life for themselves and their employees.

Shift Perceptions

Picture this: A man and a woman enter a room together and sit down on one side of the table to negotiate a business deal. The lead negotiator on the opposing side, looks at the man and asks what the initial offer is. The man calmly looks at the lead negotiator, "You'll have to ask her. She's the boss." This scenario occurs because too many people have the perception that women are not in leadership positions. Maybe they have never heard of or met a woman boss or perhaps they don't think a woman can be a leader. Regardless, we need to shift their perceptions – one dinosaur at a time.

Power dynamics, perceived or real, are expressions of how one person, or entity, holds more power and influence over another. These dynamics are often shaped by socialized viewpoints of what norms are or should be. We assume power dynamics exist in ways that conform with our own experiences. But those assumptions are sometimes subconscious and unintentional. Other times individuals purposefully view the world around them, and the people in it, through their own outdated notions about what socially acceptable power dynamics look like.

Sly and I launched our consulting firm, Wickham James Strategies & Solutions in the fall of 2019 to much fanfare and media attention. In fact, the headline in the *Kansas City Business Journal* read, "Sly James Goes into Business with his Ex-Chief of Staff (And She Gets Top Billing)." It was Sly's idea to put my name first. "You made me look better than I deserved for eight years," he said, "so now it's your turn."

Ever since we opened the consulting firm, we noticed an unforeseen catch-22. People contact me for administrative tasks, like leaving Sly a message or checking his schedule, and yet it's my name that's first on the letterhead. At first when this happened, I would take care of whatever administrative matter the caller requested. But as time went on, I realized my own behavior was playing into those socialized norms, and I was doing myself a disservice. Even Sly told me that it wasn't helpful to my own brand for me to handle those tasks, and so I made a conscious effort not to. I'm not his assistant, I'm his partner. Now when those calls come in, I connect them directly with Sly by giving them his email or phone number. Some people still seem puzzled when I tell them that I don't manage Sly's calendar. Shifting social norms does take time.

The reality is that some people aren't socialized to think Sly and I are equal partners. His stature as an elected official and his very public profile was higher than mine. This incongruence in stature probably accounts for some of this behavior. It's interesting to ponder how the situation would differ if Sly's business partner was a man. His first Chief of Staff was male, and we remained friends after he left the Mayor's office. Out of curiosity, once I became Chief of Staff, I asked him if he received calls and emails asking him to schedule a meeting for Sly. He usually didn't, but it would happen to me several times a week.

A friend of mine, a male partner at a large law firm, once told me that he noticed a difference in how he's treated versus a female colleague when they leave a meeting to see a kid's soccer game or dance recital. "People look at me like I'm a hero, when I'm really just being a parent," he explained. "My female colleague is parenting too, but because she's a woman, she gets eye rolls when she leaves for that soccer game." He overheard someone say that it was "great to see a dad babysitting." We both saw the incongruity in that remark.

Another friend was in a workplace that also needed a shift in its dealing with working parents. He was in middle management at an accounting firm and made an effort to be a real partner to his ex-wife when it came to raising their children. However, his supervisor had a hefty dose of toxic masculinity. When my friend left the office to pick up a sick child, his supervisor chastised him for "choosing snotty noses over clients." On another occasion, he went to his daughter's preschool graduation and was told, "If you had a wife, you wouldn't be guilted into doing all this."

Family responsibilities are still too often viewed as a distraction in today's workforce. Both mothers and fathers have a duty and desire to take part in their children's lives and should be supported by their employer to do so. In a hyper-connected world like ours where, thanks to our digital devices, many workers can never actually escape work. Therefore, organizations have no reason not to embrace work-life integration. Additionally, the workplace should realize that not every worker has the same access to basic needs, such as transportation and childcare. During my childhood, it was enough of a struggle for my Grandma Peterson to make it to Hardee's for the breakfast shift at 4 a.m., and she had her own car and only had to deal with rural traffic.

During the last half of our mayoral administration, Mark Nevins of The Dover Group and I were meeting with a group to garner their support for our infrastructure bond election, and we walked into a room where, as usual, I was the only woman. When the conversation began, one of the older white men looked at me straight in the eye and asked if I was taking notes because his administrative assistant was out of the office that day. Mark chimed up before I could even formulate a response. "I'll do it – the Mayor's Chief of Staff doesn't need to take notes," he said. His comment recalibrated those power dynamics – at least for the rest of the meeting.

Women involved in our campaigns frequently told me how much they enjoyed working with Mark. His support of women included those in various roles of our campaign operation – not just the Mayor's Chief of Staff. The fact that women often made a point to say something to me about how nice it was to work with a respectful man on a political campaign highlighted how uncommon it was.

From the board room to politics to dynamics within our own families, social norms are the result of generational behaviors. Those behaviors weren't formed overnight, and it's not practical to expect them to reverse with the snap of our fingers. However, the focused and deliberate action of men and women will hopefully keep future generations from following the same biased, gendered patterns.

Chapter 7

Congrats! You May Have *Something* in Common With An A-Lister

*H*ave you ever said any of the following sentences, or anything like them?

"I know I'm not ready for that promotion."

"I'm not qualified to run for elected office."

"Other people in my office have more to offer than I do."

"Someone is going to figure out that I don't know what I'm doing."

I bet that from time-to-time, all of us have had these self-doubts or ones pretty similar. Those statements are textbook examples of impostor syndrome and even successful, high-profile individuals may experience it. Megan Dalla-Camina is a strategist and author focusing on women, leadership, and well-being. She offered this definition for impostor syndrome in *Psychology Today*: "… a pattern of behavior where people doubt their accomplishments and have a persistent, often internalized fear, of being exposed as a fraud." People with impostor syndrome tend to have an inner narrative that tells them any success they have is due to luck, a lack of other qualified candidates, or even a total fluke. Additionally, impostor syndrome can creep into our minds when we begin thinking that we must meet every single criterion and know every detail before we can accomplish a task. We see this often when women leaders consider applying for a promotion or running for elected office.

Men experience impostor syndrome, too, but research suggests that men and women experience it in different ways. In 2018, *Elvesier* published a study by a team of English and German researchers that showed impostor syndrome may have worse effects on men than women. The reason? Gendered norms and stereotypes create conditions where women aren't expected to succeed at the same rate as men. So, when men do fail to meet expectations, whether it be their own or expectations placed on them by others, they tend to experience harsher feelings of failure. According to the study, "Although impostor feelings were overall higher among women, this harsh feedback seemed to especially affect male students with high impostor feelings – they reported higher anxiety, made less effort (as measured by time taken on the task), and showed a trend towards poorer performance, as compared to others given positive feedback."

The study also showed an interesting, yet concerning, contrast for female students with high impostor feelings. Instead of performing poorly to the harsh feedback, the women increased their efforts and exhibited a "superior performance." Impostor syndrome is deep-seated. When compared to their male colleagues with impostor syndrome, women tried harder, but continued feeling like impostors. For women, impostor syndrome is a stubborn culprit that can keep them from even attempting to reach positions of leadership.

But impostor syndrome doesn't have to make us stagnant, and we don't need to be paralyzed by fear. There are six strategies we can use to combat impostor syndrome:

- Share stories of experiences with impostor syndrome.
- Listen to the truth from your tribe: honest, constructive feedback.
- Banish self-doubt and overcome fear.
- Position yourself to win.
- Be someone else's support system.
- Tell your own success story.

Sharing Stories

Sharing stories about how we've all dealt with impostor syndrome from time to time helps us understand it's a common feeling, particularly when we're considering taking on new challenges or situations. The more we share our own experiences with impostor syndrome, the less isolated we'll feel. As I've observed women in leadership and how they respond to high-profile situations, I've been stunned at how many seemingly confident women have admitted to feelings of impostor syndrome. No matter how accomplished we are and how high we climb, we fall occasionally into the habit of feeling like we're a fraud. Sharing our experiences and stories reinforces that we're not alone, and maybe gives us the push to take a minute to evaluate our own self-worth. Michelle Obama, Mindy Kaling, and Penelope Cruz are three women who have openly shared their stories of impostor syndrome.

While the former first lady was named the world's "Most Admired Woman" more than once by Gallup polls, Michelle Obama has talked very candidly about her own struggles with impostor syndrome. When she made international headlines in 2018 speaking at an all-girls' school in London, Mrs. Obama referenced her modest upbringing in working-class southside Chicago. She felt that her identity as a black woman required her to represent, and almost "perform" for her entire race. She battled gender stereotypes during her legal career, which also contributed to her feelings of "I don't belong here."

Mindy Kaling's resume lists actress, comedian, writer, executive producer and director, but she still struggles with confidence. Her essay in the August 2014 issue of *Glamour* is a great read for everyone, male or female, who has had trouble with confidence. In it, she admits, "like everyone else, I have had moments when I felt unattractive and stupid and unskilled." She developed a guide dedicated to helping readers increase their confidence. Mindy Kaling credits bravery and hard work as the two keys to increasing confidence, which can lead to "the good kind" of entitlement. When I first read this, I was surprised at how Mindy Kaling, someone who seems so naturally secure and hilarious to boot, could have ever struggled with confidence. Impostor syndrome happens to many of us, irrespective of our accomplishments, intelligence or fame.

Another famous celebrity, Penelope Cruz, was signed by an agent when she was fifteen, starred in television shows and movies, and was nominated for an Emmy, Golden Globes and Oscars. She won the Oscar for best supporting actress in 2009's *Vicky Cristina Barcelona.* A celebrated beauty, Penelope Cruz has modeled for brands including L'Oréal, Ralph Lauren and Chanel. But she's no stranger to impostor syndrome. In fact, in a 2017 interview with *the Cut*, she said her impostor syndrome is so pronounced that she often feels as if she's going to be fired during the first week she's working on a project.

Understanding that women like Michelle Obama, Mindy Kaling, and Penelope Cruz experience – and talk openly – about impostor syndrome can be helpful to see that it doesn't need to stop you in your tracks. For many of us, telling our stories is a part of growing our skills, navigating new experiences, and stepping up to lead. But it's only one step to overcoming impostor syndrome. One that we continuously need to work on.

One evening in the fall of 2019, my phone rang off the hook and texts were lighting it up like Christmas lights. I was in the kitchen making dinner, and my hands were covered with flour so I couldn't pick it up. Vivian looked at it and said, "I think you won something, Mommy." I had just been named one of the Top 50 Most Powerful People in Kansas City by *Kansas City Magazine.* I thought it was a little ironic that I learned of the news while cooking dinner, no makeup on and my hair in a messy bun! Fred loved the fact that Patrick Mahomes, the Kansas City Chiefs' quarterback, was also on the list – though there's not much in common between me and the MVP of Super Bowl LIV!

My initial reaction to this news was, "How odd! How would *Kansas City Magazine* even know who I am? Why would they pick me to be one of the Top 50?" Fred looked at me incredulously. Even after talking for years about women's leadership, impostor syndrome, and self-confidence I still don't always see myself the way others do, and this experience was a classic example of that.

Truth from your Tribe: Honest, Constructive Feedback

You need people around you who will give you the honest, unfiltered feedback. This type of support system helps reframe your self-image and separate perception from reality.

Cindy Circo called me during the late fall of 2018 to tell me that she was nominating me for the Mel Carnahan Public Service Award. This annual award goes to the individual demonstrating excellence in public service and helping improve the lives of Missourians. I immediately told her I could never win, and that she should nominate Sly instead. Her response told me that I had once again fallen into the impostor syndrome trap. "Stop undervaluing yourself and your own contributions," she said. "And send me your updated resume ASAP for the application!" I sent Cindy my updated resume and somehow, I won the award along with Sara Parker Pauley, Director of the Missouri Department of Conservation. Sara was so gracious the night we accepted the award. She extended a kind acknowledgement of my accomplishment by saying that she has hope for the future of women leaders by knowing that I stand by her side.

On another occasion, I felt completely out of my league when I was in negotiations with real estate attorneys and developers who wanted to build a new convention hotel in Kansas City. I was the only person in the room without a law degree and had little experience in complex real estate transactions. I was anxious and felt sick to my stomach when a meeting was scheduled. "Everyone there must see me as a complete idiot," I told a colleague. He was a member of my tribe and helped me realize that they needed my communications expertise to navigate the tricky political dynamics on the City Council and the barrage of negative headlines. I may not have been a subject matter expert on capitalized interest or construction costs, but no one in those negotiations knew politics and public relations better than I did. My colleague suggested that I buy a real estate law book for first-year law students and familiarize myself with some of the concepts I was hearing. I read it from cover to cover and then had a good understanding of the basics. When I returned to the meetings, it was with greater confidence in the subject matter and awareness of the value I brought to those discussions.

Your tribe can be an effective tool in helping you understand when your fears and lack of confidence are adding up to impostor syndrome and creating roadblocks to your success. They can be the voice of reason that reminds you that fear is natural and often a valid response. AND, your tribe can encourage you to keep moving forward without letting fear hold you back. Think of your tribe as a mirror. They help you see a reflection of who you really are without the distortion of impostor syndrome.

In Chapter Four, we discussed the importance of incorporating people in your tribe whom you can trust to support and challenge you, which includes holding you accountable to overcoming your fears. Recognizing those fears, and why they exist, is an important step in overcoming impostor syndrome. However, your tribe can help you remember that those fears must not control you.

Banish Self-Doubt and Overcome Fear

Self-doubt and fear are common feelings for most of us when faced with unfamiliar situations and tasks. Recognizing that you may not know the answer or exactly how to proceed does not necessarily mean you're experiencing impostor syndrome. In fact, that recognition may be based on healthy self-awareness. Impostor syndrome shows up when we feel we are unable to handle a new situation or task.

Self-doubt can be the product of many factors. Social and institutional barriers certainly exacerbate self-doubt in many women. In addition, if you are doing a "first" – like the first in the family to go to college – you can feel like you don't belong in certain settings. Perhaps it's a dinner party that involves more place settings than you knew existed. Or a wine list that's more expansive than your bourgeoning palate.

I've frequently felt out of place throughout my career. My humble upbringing in North Carolina sometimes makes me doubt my place in the room. Because there are many legacy relationships in politics, my colleagues often were able to get internships and jobs or make connections through their families. Those relationships simply didn't exist for me. Thankfully, I've been able to translate many of the lessons my background did teach me into skills and traits useful in the professional world. What I lacked in networking connections early in my career, I've tried to make up with determination and stubbornness, and certainly resilience. When I worked in the Missouri Capitol, I'd see the gorgeous, imposing dome on top of the Capitol as I'd drive up to the entry gate leading to the basement parking garage. When the attendant opened the gate, I'd catch myself sighing in relief because at least one person acted like I belonged there. I'd drive my red Jeep Liberty through the gate and walk up the stairs to my office on the second floor. I'd try to push past my feelings of impostor syndrome and do my job with confidence, until I genuinely felt like I belonged there.

The business world can have a similar dynamic. Its culture can be foreign to anyone unfamiliar with it. And its hierarchical framework for upward mobility and leadership is daunting to anyone not familiar with the corporate organization and standards. An intern I knew at the Missouri Capitol decided to jump into the world of finance. She had a great resume, complete with a background in political fundraising, financial compliance, project management and organizational leadership. However, she wasn't prepared for the culture of Wall Street, and they weren't prepared for her. The firm she joined consistently told her that "her cultural deficits" and "nonconforming attitude" inhibited her performance. There could have been some truth to the fact that she had trouble assimilating to the culture, if assimilation was what they expected. Her experience taught me something: Organizations purporting to value assimilation over diversity fail to leverage the very insights an outside perspective brings. This rejection and blatant discrimination magnify an individual's self-doubt while diminishing the organization's potential. The young woman didn't give up on her goal to have a Wall Street career. She found a firm that valued her expertise as well as her unique perspective. This firm encouraged her to authentically lead her division – assimilation to outdated norms were not expected.

We can't let impostor syndrome be a self-fulfilling prophecy. If you constantly see yourself as an impostor, then you're more likely to fail. Self-doubt is a flame that fuels the fire of fear. So, how do you make a realistic plan to address your fears and move past them? First, reflect on why your fear is present. Maybe you're attempting something that's outside your comfort zone or perhaps your success would mean hitting a stereotype or gender bias head on. Next, list the skills or traits you can build to overcome your fear. Don't get overwhelmed if this list is longer than you thought it would be. Remember that as a leader, you must be continually learning in order to adapt and reframe your thinking. The list of skills you need to build so that you can overcome your self-doubt are growth opportunities. Finally, give yourself a deadline for implementing those new skills or traits. Incorporating a deadline is a good way to hold yourself accountable.

I saw this strategy work for a young woman I supervised in the Mayor's Office. I was scheduled to speak about women's leadership and the power of mentorship at a seminar she was coordinating. A communications crisis popped up at the last minute that I had to handle, and I asked her to speak in my place. She was visibly uncomfortable at the thought of public speaking. Her eyes teared up and her hands were shaking. "I've never done anything like this before, and I'm not sure I can do this," she said.

She was new to public speaking and her anxiety was in the way.

But she was passionate about the topic of women's leadership and had been the point person on our mentorship program at City Hall, so she was certainly not a novice on the subject matter. We discussed all the reasons why she was qualified to speak on the topic and reviewed the talking points and public-speaking techniques. In the end, she was a fantastic speaker, and the participants loved hearing her first-hand experiences with the mentorship program. Once that first speaking opportunity was behind her, she was comfortable seeking other speaking engagements. She later moved on to an advocacy role in the Missouri and Kansas State legislatures, and frequently found herself speaking at press conferences, legislative hearings, and community events. Without a doubt, she conquered her fear of public speaking and became a leader throughout the region on issues important to her.

What happens once you've made a plan to overcome your fears, but it still fails? You can't let the failure define you. When you find yourself in a situation where you've missed the mark, consider the lessons you've learned along the way rather than focusing on failure.

- Did you learn a valuable negotiation tactic?
- Have you overcome a biased perception?
- Did you learn a new skill or make a new contact?
- Or did an adversary show you how to message an issue in a way you hadn't considered before?

Sometimes you have to redefine success in order to process the real lesson at hand.

Position Yourself to Win

It's very difficult to be a successful leader without knowing how to communicate your vision. Many leaders fumble critical opportunities when a call to action isn't communicated properly. Communication should not be an afterthought. On the contrary, position yourself to win by prioritizing message development.

Early in my career, I observed a new leader of a civic organization engage in a strategic planning process. He believed that the organization needed to re-examine how it aligned its values with its mission and strategies. This type of reflection is a common and acceptable way for leaders to keep their organizations operating efficiently and with an eye toward the future. However, his problem was that he didn't communicate effectively with his board or staff about why he felt this strategic planning process was necessary at that time. Furthermore, he didn't tell them why the sweeping changes he was recommending were necessary for the organization's evolution. His strategic planning work, and accompanying recommendations, were met with staunch resistance and confusion. He then had to spend months educating the board and staff about his vision for the organization before he could begin implementing the recommendations from the strategic planning process. Had he communicated with his board and staff first about why his vision and supporting actions were important, he would have saved time and preserved some credibility. After this experience, he felt he was out of his league and didn't belong in a leadership position. He did have the leadership skills to guide this organization. He just skipped a very important step: communication.

Communication starts with message development. The tactics of message development vary depending on your call to action and the dynamics of your audience. However, one important constant is establishing a values-based vision with concrete expectations and metrics for success. Leaders must rally others around their vision for their organization and articulate expectations for the future based on clear values and associated metrics for success.

Important questions to consider in this message development are:

- How would you describe your vision for your organization?
- Why should others care about your vision?

- What values does your vision represent?
- What qualitative and quantitative expectations should individuals within the organization have as they do the work to implement your vision?
- How will members of your organization know when they've met or exceeded these expectations?
- How often will expectations and metrics for success be evaluated?
- How will the target audience know their actions have led to the result they want to see?

Many leaders overcomplicate the concept of taking action and fake themselves out with impostor syndrome. If you see this dynamic in your own experience, then refocus away from perceived failure and toward your call to action. You have an idea of what you want to accomplish. You just have craft the right message and present it with authority, so that the people around you embrace your vision. Once you do that, you're already gearing your organization – or community – for forward movement.

Another way to position yourself to win is to establish trust and confidence with the individuals within your organization. This means modeling behavior showing you are a leader who takes action, drives change, and gets results. The more your actions say, "I'm here to get things done. Let's do this together," the more likely you are to be a successful leader.

Here are three strategies to help you accomplish this step:

Have transparent expectations for the team.

People need to know what is expected of them so they can be effective in accomplishing the goals that are set. This transparency also generates buy-in from your team, which can speed up the systems change process. The logistics of communicating transparent expectations will differ depending on your organization's dynamics as well as what you're trying to accomplish. For example, if you're managing a team and want to ensure everyone knows the expectations for their role, then a detailed job description is needed. If you're trying to change your organization's longstanding processes, then be sure to articulate why the change is needed and re-tool your strategies for evaluating outcomes.

Establish accountability and offer redirection.

Unfortunately, not every project, employee or initiative succeeds. Redefining failure can help underscore that there are lessons in every attempt at success, regardless of the outcome. However, accountability and redirection must also come into the equation in order to build the trust and confidence of your team. This does not mean anyone should be ridiculed, but leaders must do the hard work of managing people who don't meet expectations and evaluating efforts that fail or fall short.

Accountability is required for the organization to move past the issue. Take time to consider if expectations weren't met because of a process issue, leadership issue, or something different all together. Will you continue the effort at all or recalibrate expectations? This accountability is important for individuals within your organization to see that the expectations are real and will be measured. I've seen many organizations suffer because there was no accountability for getting results. This is damaging for employee morale and for moving the organization's mission forward in a sustainable way.

Think of redirection as hitting a reset button. This allows everyone to redirect their thinking and efforts into solving the problem at hand and getting results, rather than focusing on failure. During this stage, remind your colleagues about why this work is taking place. Remind them of the mission of the organization and your vision for accomplishing the job.

Dedicate yourself to the organization's mission.

No matter what leadership position you hold, it's important to remember that the focus is not about you. It's about the organization's mission and the people working to achieve that mission. If you've ever worked with a leader who is all about himself or herself, then you know how crippling that kind of person can be to everyone and everything around them.

These egoists alienate their colleagues with their attitude. Furthermore, if the organization is successful at achieving its goals, then it's typically by accident or because of someone else's work. It's pretty difficult to be strategic if you're guided by your own ego.

Egoists tend to leave leadership vacuums in their wake. While they focus on misguided priorities, like having their face on camera or being seen in a room full of important people, the real work of leadership is usually left undone or, in some cases, is absorbed by others. While the egoists are making decisions based on their own interests, the organization's mission is put at risk. I saw this happening with the president of a non-governmental organization, or NGO. He spent so much time traveling to raise his own personal profile, rather than the NGO's mission, that he didn't manage the internal fiscal issues bubbling up within the organization. Funders took notice and threatened to stop supporting the cause unless a leadership change took place. The board finally replaced him with a leader who doubled their fundraising within twenty-four months.

When you're positioning yourself for leadership success, also consider the balance between admitting what you don't know, both to yourself and others, and embracing continuous learning. If you're geared towards feelings of impostor syndrome, then this can be especially tricky. Some of us already don't feel like we belong in a leadership position, so admitting that we don't have all the answers can further exacerbate those feelings. I've often thought to myself, "if I can't figure this out, then everyone will see that I'm not cut out for this job." But no one has every answer all the time – that's simply an unrealistic expectation.

Rather, remember that continuous learning and crowdsourcing solutions and ideas help build your own skills and the capacity of your organization. Also remember that just because you don't have all the answers doesn't mean that you're not leadership material. It just means you have an opportunity to grow. In her book *Mindset: The New Psychology of Success*, Stanford Psychologist Carol Dweck studied and wrote about how our mindset can predict success. She categorizes mindset into two distinct spaces: fixed mindset and growth mindset.

According to her research, a fixed mindset is one that assumes factors like intelligence and character can't evolve or grow. Basically, it's a belief that we're born with all the intelligence and character that we'll ever possess. On the opposite side is a growth mindset. This is a recognition that failure can lead to growth and opportunity, and that challenges are something to be welcomed, not feared.

As you hone your leadership skills and recognize that you will not always have every answer, you must let go of any tendencies to have a fixed mindset and instead embrace a growth mindset. On top of being good for your own mental health, it also sends the right message to others within your organization.

Dr. Leanna Depue, Director of the Highway Safety Division at the Missouri Department of Transportation, taught her staff this lesson frequently. During the time that I worked for her, everyone in the field considered her to be the quintessential subject matter expert on highway safety research and policy. She held a Ph.D. and her expertise was sought out by several national organizations, boards and commissions. However, she made a point to seek out her staff's input on a variety of decisions. For example, when preparing a report for the Missouri Highways and Transportation Commission, she frequently asked her staff for input on the recommendations that came from our division. Certainly, she had the expertise to develop those recommendations on her own, but that wasn't her way. Staff would say, "You're the expert, Leanna!" Her response was, "But that doesn't mean I know everything – I don't!"

Be Someone's Support System

Now that you know what impostor syndrome is, you can spot it in others and help them overcome it. Think of the people in your sphere of influence and the type of relationship you have with them. Look for first-generation professionals, individuals from underrepresented demographics within your organization, and anyone whose behaviors suggest his or her confidence is shaky. You could be their mentor, sponsor or some combination of roles. How can you encourage them in difficult situations to push past their fears and grow their confidence?

However, be careful to recognize a common situation: you are the support system for someone experiencing impostor syndrome and then that individual gives you all the credit for their success. I saw this scenario unfold when a female political candidate trounced a long-time incumbent in a State Senate election. She had been the underdog and was outspent 2 to 1. But the vote margin was so dramatically in her favor on election night, it only took a little more than an hour for pundits to give her the victory. In her speech that evening, she credited everyone from her staff, to her parents and even the weather and traffic flow for her success. After her speech, I congratulated her on her hard work. "Oh thanks, but this is just a fluke. If it wasn't for the political consultants on my team I would have never won," she said. She couldn't see her own role in her huge victory. Later that evening, she again suggested that her consultant team "gave her the victory." Thankfully, a member of her team corrected her and said a consultant team only helps highlight what the candidate represents. It was the candidate's own vision that resonated with voters that day.

Being intentional about serving as a support system for others has the added bonus of building your confidence and honing your leadership. Knowing that you helped someone else overcome their own impostor syndrome can help you see yourself as a leader and mitigate your feelings of inadequacy.

Tell Your Own Success Story

"Talking about yourself is unbecoming." That was the advice my tenth-grade English teacher gave our class. Maybe that's where my disdain for talking about myself, and my accomplishments, started. Or perhaps it was engrained earlier than that.

Dr. Deborah Tannen has studied the intersection between gender bias and communication for decades. She wrote about the power of bragging in the September-October 1995 edition of the *Harvard Business Review*. Not only does her study examine dynamics present when some of today's leaders were growing up, but it was a landmark analysis that started others in the field, and policymakers, to think about solutions to gender bias. In this article, she writes about how men and women are socialized differently, even as children, when it comes to boasting about their achievements.

"Girls learn to downplay ways in which one is better than the others and to emphasize ways in which they are all the same." Tannen wrote. Girls are taught that sounding too confident will make them unpopular. Girls will ignore the girl who calls attention to herself; they will criticize her and call her bossy. Tannen concludes "girls learn to talk in ways that balance their own needs with those of others – to save face for one another in the broadest sense of the term." Boys, on the other hand, tend to play differently. They usually play in large groups, but not everyone is treated equally. Boys with a higher group status are expected to brag rather than downplay their accomplishments. "Boys generally don't accuse one another of being bossy," Tannen observed, "because the leader is expected to tell lower-status boys what to do."

These dynamics and biases continue to exist well into adulthood and the workplace. Have you ever refrained from talking about a success because you didn't want to come off as a "know-it-all?" Or maybe you didn't want to be seen as a "bragger?" There's a good chance your decision to de-emphasize your accomplishments and success is because of the way you were socialized. Get your parents' or teachers' voices out of your head and tell others about your success.

Words, and how you speak them, also matter in communicating your success story. Tannen's research highlights how the differences in the way men and women speak can impact how they talk about success. "Men tend to be sensitive to the power dynamics of interaction, speaking in ways that position themselves as one up and resisting being put in a one-down position by others. Women tend to react more strongly to the rapport dynamic, speaking in ways that save face for others and buffering statements that could be seen as putting others in a one-down position." Today's workplace sees these linguistic patterns every day. You've likely observed this frequently without even realizing it.

I observed this very dynamic while watching a woman facilitate one group of civic leaders through a strategic-planning exercise while a man facilitated another group through the same exercise. She encouraged ideas from almost everyone in her group, while he took feedback from the usual suspects – the people who talk to fill the air. When the two groups came together to report their findings, he said "I" or "my group's findings" whereas the woman used the pronoun, "we" and spoke about, "our group's findings." As the session ended, I overheard people rave about the man's performance, but rarely anyone commented on her performance. The words we use, especially the pronouns we choose in a sentence, can be reflective of how our brains are conditioned to communicate.

Both men and women can unknowingly play a role in perpetuating a damaging cycle that negatively affects women. During childhood, socially conditioned norms, like career guidance steering girls away from math and sciences, was evident for many of us and society at-large. Then as adults, we often subconsciously perpetuate these flawed or demeaning stereotypes by our communication or actions. Our own word choices and actions can further the cycle and continue the stereotypes. The cycle looks like this:

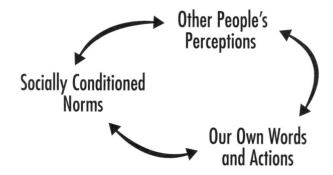

Breaking this cycle is not easy, particularly when many of the actions involved in the cycle are subconscious. Honest reflection from both men and women about the roles we play in the cycle is the first step to breaking it. Once we know how we've contributed to the cycle, then we can change our actions and our outlook accordingly.

As I was writing this chapter conclusion, I reviewed the chapter from the beginning. Did you notice the way I wrote about winning the Mel Carnahan Public Service Award? I wrote that I "somehow" won. Impostor syndrome sneaks in even when I'm writing on how to avoid it! Don't let it sneak in on you. Sometimes you will notice it yourself, but other times it takes someone else calling it to your attention.

When you're feeling like you don't belong or you aren't good enough, remember that many of us sometimes feel the same way. You are not disqualified from being a leader just because impostor syndrome occasionally rears its head. It simply means you aren't a narcissist – and that's a good thing! Tannen's research tells us that "women are likely to downplay their certainty; men are likely to minimize their doubts." These dynamics impact how impostor syndrome manifests in our daily life. The more we recognize this, the more deliberate we can become in fighting impostor syndrome within ourselves and support others as they do the same.

Chapter 8
Emotional Intelligence: So Important, Yet in Short Supply

*H*ave you ever worked around, or observed, leaders – male or female – who frequently behaved as if they were having a meltdown? Their voice was typically loud, or the tone was harsh, and everything seemed to be a crisis. Or maybe they didn't have a handle on the nuances of the situation, and even though the clues to how others were feeling were evident, they just didn't see them. It's likely that these leaders lacked emotional intelligence. Their leadership skills were compromised because they couldn't – or wouldn't – see that their lack of understanding themselves and others kept them from getting the job done. It's also likely that their organization suffered as a result.

Emotional intelligence is the capacity for understanding our own feelings and the feelings of others, and the capacity for managing our emotions effectively in our relationships. It's also a helpful tool in motivating ourselves and others. Emotional intelligence is sometimes referred to as "people smarts." This differs from a person's IQ, or intelligence quotient, which focuses on conceptional abilities and intelligence capacity. Individuals with high IQs don't necessarily have strong emotional intelligence. And emotionally intelligent people don't always have the highest IQs.

When you can manage your own emotions and redirect the emotions of others, you're more apt to build relationships, influence decisions, and lead diverse groups. Emotional intelligence is critical to leadership. It's not always innate for everyone, but it can be learned. A good leader recognizes its importance and works toward making emotional intelligence a part of his or her skill set.

Emotional intelligence is made up of several competencies that can be studied and practiced over time. The competencies are organized into four major themes: self-awareness, self-management, social awareness, and socials skills.

Self-Awareness

I worked for a gentleman who considered himself to be a highly skilled "people manager." But the behavior he really exhibited was manipulation. As a result, he was unable to direct his employees' skills and energy into results benefitting the organization. He was not a good leader, but he certainly enjoyed telling people what to do. I learned from him that those two things are not the same. Giving orders may have cleared his to-do list, but managing employees requires more than that. He was unaware of his manipulative behavior and it was a shame for all of us, and the organization, that he lacked such self-awareness.

Self-reflection requires us to be aware of our failings and strengths and that isn't always easy to do. Take the time to list your strengths and weaknesses. Ask yourself: What makes me tick? Where do my talents lie, and where do I fall short? Recall the effective leaders you've seen. What was the key to their leadership success? How did they pivot when things didn't go as they had planned? Also, think about an ineffective leader that you've observed. What did he or she do – or not do – when the team missed a big deadline?

After making your list, think honestly about your reaction to constructive criticism. Are you hyper-sensitive? Do you recoil at the thought that you may be impatient? Are you comfortable making a plan to strengthen your listening skills? Listening to and acting on constructive criticism can make you a better leader. React negatively to criticism, and you've missed an opportunity for growth.

Learning to receive feedback and constructive criticism, and then acting on it accordingly, is important in every field. Lawyers give feedback to their clients. Political advisers give advice to elected officials. Customers give a variety of feedback to companies. In many cases, understanding what to do with that feedback could mean the difference between a promotion or remaining stagnant in the company – or worse, being fired.

Another dimension of self-awareness is recognizing how you bring your authentic self to the table. Authenticity is the quality of being real. You should know how the real YOU impacts your leadership abilities and effectiveness. Maybe you decide that humor is a tool that helps you convey your message in a way that's most effective, sincere, and comfortable. Or perhaps you leverage your tendency to be direct in your communication because anything else feels like an inefficient use of time. Whatever the case may be, knowing your authentic self and how you convey it to others, is key to self-awareness.

Working with Sly over the years, particularly in the Mayor's Office, has taught me a lot about being authentic at the workplace. Sly has a very direct communication style, which leaves no doubt as to what he's thinking, or where he is on an issue. The majority of people seemed to appreciate this about him. However, there were certainly some who were put off by it. He's often admitted that this personality trait can be a blessing and a curse. Boldly expressing his opinion is authentically him, and he accepts any consequences that may come with it. Sometimes that results in a grumpy City Council member – or two. Other times it equates to an approval rating of more than 75 percent among voters.

We may uncover some uncomfortable truths about ourselves. I know I struggle with patience – you've heard me say that before! Therefore, I'm also not always as successful as I'd like to be at motivating people who lack initiative. I can get quickly frustrated by these types of individuals, particularly when my to-do list is long. The result of this dynamic has sometimes been me thinking to myself, "I'll just do it myself." I know this isn't constructive for anyone, and I've gotten better at checking myself when I feel this urge, but it's still something I work on daily.

Self-Management

After you've taken the time to evaluate and become aware of your strengths and weaknesses, you're better able to move into self-management. This competency comes into play when you are aware of your own deficits or strengths and proactively strategize with them in mind. For instance, if your self-awareness helps you determine that you tend to jump to conclusions, then you should practice self-management skills to address that issue. Resist the urge to stop and rest at the self-awareness stage though, because your work has really only just begun.

I worked at the Missouri State Capitol with a State Senator who wanted to work on every request from her constituents, even if their requests weren't always feasible. Most of these requests involved a budget increase which is difficult to accomplish under the best circumstances. She and her staff knew that she said "yes" too often to these requests, but with good intentions. Her well-meaning "yeses" became problematic when she couldn't deliver on everything she promised and spent too much time on impractical requests. To combat this issue, she and her team developed a polite response to every request assuring constituents that options would be explored, and the Senator would get back with them on the best course of action. That tactic gave them some space to consider each request's feasibility and kept the Senator out of hot water with her constituents. The Senator's self-awareness about her desire to act on all these budget requests helped fashion a productive self-management technique. She and her team were better able to give her constituents a realistic view of how she could best help them.

I learned the value of a well-placed pause during any communication interaction by watching a tobacco-industry mogul navigate a public hearing in the North Carolina Legislature in the late 1990s. I was taking a political communication class and had to write a report on the different communications techniques exhibited by both sides during a contentious hearing. My professor told us to pay close attention to the way the tobacco executive reacted to the legislators' questions. It didn't take long to see the legislators wanted to make the executive uncomfortable and push his buttons. I assumed they wanted him to say something shocking or alarming so they could then pile on and hopefully create more unforced errors on his part. The tobacco executive remained calm and respectful and never raised his voice. At one point, I noticed that he took a brief pause before he answered the questions peppered at him. My professor explained that pausing before giving your answer after you've been asked a seemingly intrusive question can help you formulate a response that's less emotional and more advantageous to moving the conversation forward. Ending your time in the hot seat without losing your cool can save your reputation and bring a difficult situation to a resolution. I did not agree with what the tobacco company was trying to accomplish at the hearing, but I could appreciate the way the executive handled himself and conveyed his message.

We all need a buffer from time to time. Incorporating an appropriate pause into your answers when you're in an interview, a negotiation, a hearing or any format where your response will be under the microscope, is a good self-management tactic to reaffirm your composure and expertise.

Social Awareness

Being able to recognize behaviors and emotions and how they affect individuals and organizations is a powerful tool. You may have heard this referred to as "reading a room." Emotions are complex. They can sometimes be irrational, and other times, instructive on how you can best manage the past to chart a new course. There are also times when reading emotions, like joy or pride, can help you leverage a moment to drive results. Recognizing the complexity and opportunity of emotions, and then managing them, are critical parts of social awareness and leadership.

While I was Chief of Staff to the Mayor, I watched two leaders manage their reactions to similar situations. One blamed her problems with solving an issue on other people and took everything personally. The other read the room and pivoted her strategy based on the shifting dynamics she witnessed. She was able to read others' emotions and plan around them before the situation got out of hand. IQ had nothing to do with the way each of them managed their situation. It was all about their people-smarts.

As a political staffer for various offices, I've watched participants' behaviors in meetings. I wanted to read their body language, observe their reactions, and absorb the unspoken dynamics of each room. As a speechwriter, this helped me understand how audiences reacted to words and phrases. But as someone who later led negotiations, social awareness was instrumental in helping me determine how far I could take a conversation, and to what extent opposing sides could be pushed. If the person on the other side of the table was obviously tense, then I would pivot or reframe the conversation. If they were engaged in the parameters I laid out, then I would continue pushing in that direction to get the deal done.

Early in my career, one critique I received from my managers was that I didn't talk enough in meetings. I was told, "You're basically out of sight and out of mind." My managers were all men whose expectations of ideal meeting behavior were likely, subconsciously or not, framed by their own behaviors and definitions of appropriate communication techniques. What they didn't notice was that while they were busy talking, many of the meeting's participants were tuned out. I paid attention to the restlessness and doodling from the others in the room. The guys may have been talking a lot, but no one was listening.

These managers not only lacked social awareness of their surroundings, but they lacked the skill of knowing what the important points of the conversation were. Have you ever been around someone who frequently talked to fill the air? Maybe you've even said, "He loves to hear himself talk!" Knowing what information to share and when to share it is an increasingly important social skill. As attention spans shorten, due in large part to the continual rise of digital communication, maximizing the significance of your words will matter even more.

Social Skills

The fourth competency is social skills, and these are easier to maximize once you've developed greater self-awareness, self-management, and social awareness. Social skills can be honed over time and they can help you become a dynamic leader who inspires others. I'm certainly an example of how we are not born with all the social skills we will ever have. Think of these skills as a muscle. The more they're used, the stronger they are. Here are a few social skills that I believe are worth prioritizing:

Be the "Bucket Filler"

Vivian's kindergarten teacher asked her students to be a "bucket filler" for someone every day. If someone needs help, a bucket filler lends a hand without expecting anything in return. Bucket fillers are definitely leaders because they're always ready to help, even if they don't get recognition for it. Furthermore, bucket fillers know when they can take center stage and when the moment is right for them to give their support from the side of the stage.

My mother-in-law, Judy Wickham, is the quintessential bucket filler. She has five children and thirteen grandchildren. If anyone in the family needs her for something, she'll immediately drop whatever she's doing and take care of the issue at hand. She didn't work outside the home until later in life when her children were grown, and her husband had passed away. However, she's immensely supportive of the working mothers around her. The only remark she's ever made about my oftentimes erratic work schedule is to ask if I'm taking care of myself and prioritizing time alone with

Fred. She can usually tell the answer by the exhausted look on my face and then offers to hang with Viv so I can have some alone time or some couple time – or both. Judy has more energy than I've ever had – and she's forty years older. She never wants anything in return for her help because the greatest gift anyone could give her is time with her family.

She would chuckle at the idea of being a model for leadership, but she truly is. We were once joking about who her favorite child was, and she said, "It's whoever needs me the most at the moment." Years later, a staff member came to me upset because, in her view, I hadn't been giving enough attention to her project. I was reminded of Judy's quote, and I explained to her that my attention had to be given to whatever crisis was brewing at the moment. If I wasn't in her office a lot, then she should be relieved because it meant she had things under control.

Develop Empathy

Learn to put yourself in someone else's shoes. We are all going through life with different perspectives, experiences, barriers, and opportunities. Those differences shape us and inform our frames of reference. Leaders should embrace the unique contributions of others and help them maximize their potential. Empathetic leaders don't ostracize those who bring different skills to the team or who come from different backgrounds.

If you develop empathy, then you can more easily appreciate others' value to your organization. Being empathetic is closely related to showing sympathy. The difference is that showing sympathy means you feel compassion, maybe even pity, toward another person. Empathy is the ability to put yourself in someone else's position. Empathy also allows you to better connect with the people around you, which makes you a better leader in return.

I was extremely frustrated with one young man who was working with us at City Hall. His work product had been on a downward slide, and he was often late for work. He came to us with so much promise, but now was underperforming. I was ready to kick him to the curb.

At the end of a particularly rough week, I called him into my office and asked him what was going on. He told me his mother had been deported and he was helping his younger siblings figure out their "new normal" without their mother living with them. His mother was also dealing with medical challenges in Mexico, and he was trying to make sure she had access to the care she needed. He was barely coping with his personal responsibilities, and his professional ones were a low priority at the time. We talked about ways to life his burden and manage his time. He left our office at the end of our term with a new appreciation for resiliency. I am so grateful that I listened to the "mother" in me and called him into my office to talk. Being empathetic to what this young man was going through was not being weak on my part. He used his second chance to sharpen his skill set and clarify his goals. But most of all, he saw that someone was in his corner and had his back.

Be Forgiving and Truly Forget

It's so easy for humans to hold a grudge. Yet, it's so unproductive and takes too much energy. If you're able to forgive others who disappoint you or who blatantly do you wrong, then you can save your energy for more constructive endeavors.

Dr. Leanna Depue, Director of Highway Safety at the Missouri Department of Transportation, illustrates what we should all strive to be when it comes to our ability to forgive and forget. Leanna had been a leader in her field for years and was beloved by the employees within the department. She was well-respected by the Legislature as well, even among those who vehemently disagreed with her efforts to pass a primary seatbelt law and to require motorcyclists to wear helmets. The Department of Transportation announced in 2011 that it would be slashing its overhead costs so it could focus more of its resources toward building and maintaining the state's roads. No division would go without making drastic cuts and that meant layoffs. Ultimately, the Highway Safety Division was merged with another division, and Leanna's director position was eliminated through the merger process. She took a Deputy Director position and handled the gut punch with grace and professionalism.

One lesson in building an appetite for forgiveness is knowing that we all are wrong at some point. And when we are the ones who make a mistake, we will also want the benefit of forgiveness.

Admit Fault

This brings me to the next social skill that's important to emotional intelligence – admitting when you've screwed up. This is difficult for some people to do, particularly for the leaders who view admitting fault as a sign of weakness. But failing to admit fault can diminish the respect and confidence of the people around you. If they can't expect you to own up to your mistakes, then why should they embrace your vision and follow your lead?

I worked with a CEO of a hospital system who graciously and professionally accepted the blame for a security breach of their patient records. He wasn't personally responsible for any of the mismanagement leading to the breach. Considering how large the hospital system was, he may not have even personally known the individuals who were responsible. However, he appeared before the news media, the State Legislature, and his employees to apologize and outline the steps his organization was taking to ensure this never happened again. Several months later, a large communications company made the news for a similar security breach related to consumer financial information. However, the CEO publicly ridiculed his employees and even blamed the customers for having weak passwords. The two situations showed a clear contrast in leadership styles and emotional intelligence. One leader understood the power of accepting responsibility while the other missed a valuable opportunity to show emotional intelligence and chart a new course for his organization.

Comparing and contrasting socially acceptable leadership styles with the traits of emotional intelligence can reveal some gender stereotypes. For example, it's usually more socially acceptable for men to lead from a place of aggression than with emotional intelligence. Men can be considered weak if they exhibit traits related to emotional intelligence, like empathy. On the other hand, women who use emotional intelligence in their own leadership may be praised for leading with a nurturer's perspective when they exhibit empathy. Or they may be accused of leaning toward the Cupcake side of the thin line. Incorporating emotional intelligence into leadership development can help break down these false assumptions for both men and women.

Better understanding the link between emotional intelligence and leadership can also help men and women develop executive presence. Even if you haven't heard the term executive presence before, you've likely observed it – or the lack of it. You see it when a person walks into a room with confidence, uses effective communication and everyone in the room pays attention. A leader without executive presence will struggle to give direction even to a heated conversation. You can also achieve an executive presence by avoiding giving contradictory signals like slouching, speaking timidly or by failing to properly read the dynamics of the room.

Executive presence is the ability to lead and convey power based on physical presence, communication presence and emotional presence. Both men and women can struggle with executive presence, but women are more likely to be penalized for lacking it. This is primarily due to societal biases about women's appearances and behaviors. Gender bias can be improved to some degree by focusing on how we present ourselves in the three areas of executive presence: physical presence, communication presence, and emotional presence.

Physical Presence

Fair or not, people notice your physical presence first. Many times, I have walked into a negotiation or a contentious hearing and noticed men and women looking me up and down. My stature and relative youth immediately make some people, consciously or not, underestimate my ability to handle tough situations. I recognize that my height and age may be a liability, so I make a point to dress the part of a leader. Interestingly enough, other women can be critical of this tactic. I've been told that, "It shouldn't matter how you dress!" and "You're diminishing your own intellect by dressing in a suit all the time!" or "You're using your sexuality to score points!" But I see it differently.

Sometimes my stature, physical appearance, even my southern accent, is an asset. Other times, any of these qualities can erode my confidence in certain settings and negatively influence how others view my experience and expertise. So, I've decided that what works best for me is to bring my best self to each situation in a way that feels most authentic for me. In a business setting, that usually means a suit, heels, jewelry, and lipstick – the whole nine yards. Knowing your audience helps determine how much latitude you may get with physical presence. For example, I know that I am not likely to build credibility with CEOs if I show up to a meeting in leggings and Converse shoes. But if I go to a townhall meeting to discuss early childhood education with young families, then showing up in something less than a tailored suit is fine.

Your physical presence won't translate as confidence or power if it isn't authentic to your personality and values. If it translates at all, it's likely to be in awkwardness and insincerity. It's important to strike a balance between presenting yourself in a manner that instills confidence and credibility among those you need to influence AND still feels authentic to your own values. Finding this balance takes equal doses of self-reflection and practice.

Communication Presence

This component of executive presence reflects how well you connect with others. Many studies have been conducted on the power of communication in leadership. The result is that about 90 percent of a leader's communication is nonverbal, including things like eye contact, posture, and even physical appearance.

Political candidates are often surprised by how much time is spent learning how to stand or considering what clothes to wear during debate preparation. It's because so much authority and executive presence is conveyed by nonverbal communication. The hard truth is that more often than we'd like to admit, leaders must earn the right to be heard by their followers. If your body language doesn't convey authority, then you aren't likely to convey your expertise through verbal communication.

A female CEO of a Fortune 500 company told me that she practiced every ounce of bad news she had to deliver to employees or clients in front of a mirror before she actually delivered the message. She started this practice so that she could see how she herself reacted to certain words. If she thought she fell short of delivering the news effectively, she could pivot her voice or posture. She wanted her nonverbal message to complement the verbal message so that there would be no question what she meant.

The delivery of your message becomes easier to navigate once you've established authority through physical presence and nonverbal communication. You can better formulate your ideas to match your audience and align your goals accordingly once the people you're trying to influence accept your authority.

As you deliver your message, other communication strategies will come into play like active listening and extemporaneous interactions. Even at the highest levels of leadership, communication is a two-way street. The more you actively listen in conversations, the better equipped you'll be to respond and act strategically. This means paying attention to how people react while you're speaking.

Bill Clinton and Ronald Reagan were legendary on the campaign trail for making audience members feel as if they were having an intimate conversation with them. That's because they were careful to watch the audience for specific reactions and then feed off them, even singling out some bystanders for effect.

Emotional Presence

Emotional presence is how well emotional intelligence competencies show up in times of stress. If leaders can't demonstrate self-management qualities, then they will probably have a difficult time convincing anyone else that they have the skills to manage an entire organization, or even deserve the opportunity to try.

I'll never forget trying to coach an executive of a global company before he testified in front of a group of elected officials at a hearing. It was soon evident that he rejected any sort of constructive criticism or feedback. He was used to being in charge and making the rules. He was not comfortable having to ask for permission or explaining his decisions. This outlook, combined with a bunch of politicians with a populist tilt, was a recipe for disaster.

The executive's testimony was curt and dismissive. He was righteously indignant for most of the hearing. Even in media interviews, he came off as abrasive and with a short fuse. If he was a woman, the word "unhinged" would have been used to describe him. His physical presence certainly looked the part, and his talking points were on-message and clear. But his emotional presence was so poor that none of it mattered.

After the hearing, I went from office to office trying to undo the damage he had done to himself and the project. One of the elected officials said, "He is about as centered as my three-year-old grandson." I couldn't disagree.

Later that evening, I went home and had dinner with Vivian, who was in kindergarten at the time. She was telling me how she was learning the importance of "belly breathing" from her teacher when she was upset. Belly breathing is a calming exercise to regulate one's emotions and help find the appropriate words to communicate. Vivian showed me how she took the deep breaths. It was a striking contrast to the behavior I witnessed at the hearing earlier that day. Sometimes, we forget the leadership basics we should've learned as kindergartners.

Luckily, people aren't born with all the emotional intelligence they'll ever have. It can be built and refined. The only requirement is a desire for growth and a willingness to evolve – and even to learn from a kindergartener.

Chapter 9
Are You a *Cupcake,* a *Bitch,* or Maybe *Both?*

I **was barely twenty-five** years old when I landed the opportunity to meet with the Speaker of the House to discuss pending legislation that was before the Missouri House of Representatives. From my perspective as a young woman just beginning her career at the State Capitol, the Speaker was the epitome of power. He not only held the key to making public policy happen in the state, but he was also a successful and prolific fundraiser for himself and his party. All the political pundits said his career path was only headed in one direction: upward. And he walked with a certain swagger that exuded confidence.

After days of preparing for this meeting, I walked into his office ready for anything – or so I thought. After his legislative aide greeted me, she took me into his office where I sat on a couch looking at plaques, trophies, and family photographs, including those of his two daughters. It seemed like an hour before the Speaker arrived, but once he did, he looked me up and down and gave me a smirk as he walked to the chair behind his desk. "Honey, I'd love to talk to you about your stuff, but first you're going to have to come over here and sit on my lap," he said, flashing the whitest teeth I'd ever seen. I was mortified, scared to death, and shocked. "What would you do if someone spoke to your daughters like that? You can go to hell!" I yelled as I collected my belongings and left his office.

When I told a few colleagues about what happened, I received feedback that I wasn't expecting. One person thought I was overly bitchy to him. Another suggested I should have been nicer when I told him how inappropriate his behavior was. Others even thought

I should have completely let it slide and just concentrate on getting my work done. In their view, I would be the one to blame if I had angered him badly enough for our agenda to be derailed. But I didn't see that interaction as the time and place for Cupcake mode. I'm not sure if I could have lived with myself had I just shrugged it off with a smile or allowed his improper advances to continue.

Not every situation is as cut and dry as my encounter with the Speaker. I quickly chose my reaction, landing solidly on one side of the line between Cupcake and Bitch. Chances are you've experienced that thin line and felt less sure where to stand. What situations require the Cupcake? The Bitch? Should you care which one you are perceived to be? What exactly does it mean to be perceived as a Cupcake? A Bitch? Can you be both? There are many factors to consider, and it can be difficult to have honest conversations with yourself and others to determine how the line affects you. It's not always feasible to plan for every scenario, but it's wise to think through how your actions are perceived, if they position you for success, and if they help dismantle gender bias or play into it.

To Care or Not to Care

When I hear someone say, "I don't care what other people think of me," I often wonder how true that statement is. Most people do care how they're viewed, whether they want to admit it or not. And if they truly don't care at all, then they probably struggle with self-awareness and have work to do in order to be a more effective leader.

If you care about getting results, then you should care about how the people around you receive your communication and your leadership style. This is not the same thing as compromising your values or changing your vision to conform to a stereotype or social norm. It definitely doesn't mean you must accept behavior that makes you feel uncomfortable or puts you in harm's way, like sexual harassment. Reflecting on how you interact with others and how your leadership style gets results can help you become a better leader. It's also important to take the time to analyze what went wrong when your leadership technique failed to deliver the results you were looking for. Doing so can also help you determine how you can improve the next time.

When I've asked other women whether we should care what others think, inevitably someone says something like this: "But if I spend time worried about how people feel about me, aren't I just playing into a patriarchal system where women are expected to tip toe around their own beliefs and personalities?" Or I'll hear, "Changing the way I act will make me fake."

My take: It's not that simple.

Understanding how you are received by others helps you shape the strategy and identify the tactics you use to lead. Once you are aware of any gaps, or maybe even areas where you excel, you can decide if you need to pivot or adapt your behavior to be more effective. The same holds true when it comes to the thin line between Cupcake and Bitch.

Cupcake

Here's a little secret. You do not have to like someone to work with them. Grandma Chamblee would say, "Working the fields with somebody doesn't mean you gotta marry him."

The hallmark of effective leadership is the ability to push beyond your own emotions and preferences and focus instead on your organization's goals. Is this considered fake or being too nice? Far from it. Rather, you're embracing Cupcake mode by putting your organization above your personal feelings and any negative history or baggage that may exist. Leaders realize their feelings about certain relationships cannot interfere in either the organization's day-to-day business or its mission.

It's impossible to enumerate all the scenarios where Cupcake might come in handy. So, you'll need to use some discernment – a trait we focused on earlier in this book – to consider if Cupcake is the leadership style best-suited for your situation. The guidelines listed below can help you determine if the Cupcake mode will be most effective. If any of the following conditions exist, then consider stepping to the Cupcake side:

- When bad blood or experiences, or negative emotions prevent others on your team from building and maintaining relationships;
- When a voice of reason, through active listening, executive presence, and emotional intelligence, is needed to focus a group on problem-solving; or,
- When interpersonal dynamics or outside forces inhibit good communication and consensus building.

Another time when Cupcake mode can be beneficial is when most people are around you are in full bitch mode. I often saw this in the Missouri Legislature where testosterone and ideology tended to rule the day over emotional intelligence and problem-solving. I found more often than not, the Capitol needed a voice of reason and Cupcake mode definitely helped.

I played the role of Cupcake to a few city councilmembers more frequently than I would have liked. There were definitely times I would have preferred to avoid a few of them altogether, but that wasn't feasible. Being more Cupcake than Bitch served a strategic purpose. I wasn't compromising my values – quite the contrary – I, along with Sly, was singularly focused on making our city better. However, a few councilmembers made it very difficult to build relationships based on trust. They were less than honest in negotiations, leaked information to the media, and even tried to impugn Sly's character. It was easier for me to summon the willpower to be a Cupcake and work with them than it was for Sly. They were personally attacking him – not me. But my goal wasn't to get even or play politics. There was work to be done, so off I'd go with a smile, a strategy, and Grandpa Chamblee's voice inside my head reminding me, "You can catch more flies with honey than vinegar."

Regardless of your industry and profession, chances are you'll run across others who are focused on "I-win-and-you-lose" strategies. But those strategies rarely lead to any sustainable, effective change in any organization. And they certainly don't help solve tough problems. In these situations, lean into skills like active listening, executive presence and emotional intelligence to calm the waters and refocus the attention on solving the problem at hand. People who employ "I-win-and-you-lose" strategies usually blow right past effective communication and message development.

Message development is also essential because many disagreements, both in politics and in the boardroom, arise and are often exacerbated by a lack of communication. I observed the merger of two large companies blow up simply because of a communications failure. Millions of dollars were wasted on the merger effort, and careers were tarnished, because the two sides were focused on "winning" rather than collaborating.

The next time someone suggests that you're a Cupcake and maybe "too nice," remember that he or she is the one with the misplaced assumptions. You're more like Ex-Lax and "making shit happen."

Bitch, Not Bitchy

You've probably heard a woman called a bitch if she's viewed as overly aggressive, mean, or just "too much." Certainly, all of us can come off more hostile than we had intended from time to time. But comments like this show that social norms and biases still exist in almost every workplace.

Bitch mode means several things. Perhaps you're facing inappropriate behavior and need to put someone in his or her place. Or maybe you're focused on results and need to push back on the extraneous behavior getting in the way. At other times, you're in a leadership position making difficult decisions not everyone will love.

Like Cupcake mode, it's difficult to list all the scenarios when you're better off channeling your inner Bitch. But here's a few examples when Bitch would be warranted:

- Rejecting harassment, discrimination, or gender bias;
- Leading while recalibrating strident, unrealistic expectations;
- Managing team dynamics and personalities.

Let's take a look at my interaction with the Speaker of the Missouri Legislature. First, he and several of my colleagues expected me to take his harassment in stride, as if it was just a working condition that came with the territory. Second, my admonishment of his behavior was surprising to several staffers at the Capitol. They considered him too powerful to have his actions corrected. Finally, his legislative aide didn't seem surprised at all by the interaction. Perhaps she'd been there before herself, or maybe she felt more comfortable in a Cupcake role. His behavior and all their reactions taught me that being a Bitch is the best way to make a point and stand up for yourself when faced with harassment, discrimination or gender bias – even if it surprises everyone around you.

When you're leading projects or people, you may find yourself occasionally needing to embrace your inner Bitch. Project management requires leaders to adhere to deadlines and expectations and to hold the team to the same. This accountability does not always jive with the perceptions and assumptions of everyone on the team.

A colleague in the event planning industry was struggling to meet the deadlines to pull off a high-profile festival. Her staff didn't seem to understand that failure to meet one deadline meant other tasks and their target dates would pile up, putting the entire event at risk. She decided to require her staff to work overtime – paid overtime – in order to catch up on their long to-do list. Some of the staff reacted poorly and told a few festival vendors that their boss was a bitch for making them work such long hours. During one-on-one meetings, my colleague told each one of the complainers that his or her unprofessional behavior was insubordinate and keeping a 9-to-5 schedule was unrealistic in the event-planning industry. Not everyone's employment in the company survived the experience, but she felt like those who remained had more realistic expectations of the industry and respected her for holding the others accountable.

A few months later, I found myself coaching a young man who told me he was unhappy in our organization because he assumed he would get to "hang out" with the mayor more. His expectations about the job were not meeting the reality of his role in relation to the mayor of a big city. Ambitious "young guns" are often dismayed when reality hits. They don't understand that trust must be built, acceptance earned, and value proven before a strong relationship can exist between a staffer and an elected official. When I explained this dynamic to the young man, he immediately became defensive, personalized my characterization, and thought I was being bitchy. His unrealistic expectations hampered his focus and showed me that he was more interested in his own ego than being a productive member of our team. Leaders need to remain focused on the goals of the organization, not coddling the team members.

Leading a team can be a rewarding experience when you're able to help people build their skill sets, see their potential, and accomplish their professional dreams. But it can be difficult when you must manage complicated team dynamics and personalities. Perhaps you've had to discipline an employee, assign them a task they didn't like, or maybe hold them accountable for poor performance. None of these supervisory tasks are fun, and while necessary, can create hard feelings and intensify complicated dynamics.

There have been days where I'd leave the office frustrated over how much time I spent dealing with office drama, rather than on moving a public policy agenda forward, solving a problem, or communicating information to stakeholders. Inevitably, it felt like a staff member was unsatisfied with how I handled one episode or another. At those times my tribe would remind me, "You don't need to be their friend. You need to be their leader." It's good advice to remember. Similarly, Sly managed one reporter's question about how he felt with the pushback he was getting from the City Council by saying, "If I wanted to be loved then I would have opened a pet store." My tribe and Sly were right that leadership requires making decisions that move the organization forward, but those decisions may not get you invited to happy hour.

Leaders cannot worry about who likes them and who doesn't. They must be focused on the mission of the organization. Decision-makers cannot make everyone happy, but they can carefully consider the positive and negative ramifications of their choices. If you're treating your employees and team with respect, guiding them professionally, and adhering to your organization's protocol, then you're doing your job. An employer, who was also a mentor, once told me, "I hired you to get the job done. I did not hire you to raise you." I remembered his admonition, especially when working with people I'd rather not meet for happy hour. Sometimes I've needed to remind myself that I don't have to like the people around me, but I do have to work with them.

If you find yourself in a situation where Bitch is more appropriate, remember that leadership is not about being liked all the time. Rather, leaders make tough decisions, focus on goals and outcomes, emphasize accountability, and make things happen. If you can do all those things and be liked by everyone around you all of the time, then you should write a book to tell the rest of us how it's done.

When Cupcake and Bitch Intersect

As I've navigated my career, I've learned that both sides of the line separating Cupcake and Bitch are necessary depending on the situation. Emotional intelligence helps us determine when we can be effective as a Cupcake, a Bitch, or something in between.

Both the Cupcake and Bitch modes are states of mind. Neither is an indictment of our actions or personalities, and neither is a defect in character or behavior. Rather, both can be a compliment if used in the correct situation. Cupcake and Bitch are two different strategies to employ in order to get something done. At face value, there is nothing wrong with either one of them. Yet, neither is optimal all the time.

Discernment is necessary to effectively choose what side of the line you should walk on, or if you should widen the line by being a little bit of both. Think about a time when you combined active listening, emotional intelligence and executive presence while making a difficult decision that you knew wouldn't make everyone happy. You likely exhibited both Cupcake and Bitch traits, resulting in some people thinking you were "too nice" and others calling you a bitch. When this happens, ask yourself if your goal was accomplished and if any part of the process was bumpier than it should have been. If you managed to accomplish your goal with a relatively smooth process, then you found an ideal spot on the line between Cupcake and Bitch for that situation. If not, take the time to be honest with yourself in assessing what didn't go as well as it could have. Maybe you had the active listening part down and even showed high emotional intelligence but lacked the executive presence to seal with deal. You now have the tools discussed in Chapter 8 to build those skills for next time. Whatever the circumstance may be, assessing what didn't go right can set you up for success when you encounter a similar situation down the road.

I've usually tried to stay on the Cupcake side of the line in professional situations. That side feels more authentic to me and tends to fit my personality most of the time. But I've learned not to be afraid of my inner Bitch. And the upside of more frequently exhibiting Cupcake traits is that when I do cross the line and become a Bitch, then people take notice. Because I use the Bitch mode relatively sparingly, it tends to make an impact when I do, and people pay attention. I've known men and women who were always overly aggressive and yes, even bitchy. Their voice and perspective lost impact because they were always mad about something. Chapter 4 has strategies to use with people who have this "mad-at-the-world" disorder.

One time I overheard a City Hall staffer talking about me, not realizing I was in the stairwell behind him. We'd been engaged in a tense meeting with some stakeholders. A couple of the meeting participants were clearly not focused on reaching a resolution and repeatedly disparaged the Mayor and the City Manager. The staff member said, "You can tell Joni is pissed when she looks someone in the eye and tells them to stop wasting her time." I was happy to overhear this. The staff member recognized that I was being patient in the meeting, but only to a point where I wouldn't let my opponents sabotage reaching a decision. Switching from one side of the line to the other in order to maximize your effectiveness is a good strategy for widening that line.

Have you ever wondered if you should try to adjust the way you act and conduct business in an attempt to widen the line between Cupcake and Bitch? My advice is to accept that we all have work to do – both men and women – in reshaping perceptions and dismantling biases about both sides of the line. We've been conditioned to view both Cupcake and Bitch in a negative context. The truth is, both are necessary.

Cupcake mode doesn't equate to being weak or passive. Who hasn't been in a situation where someone practicing active listening could have saved the day? Taking the time to listen, pause, and *then* react is a sign of strength and leadership. And Bitch mode isn't all bad. Sometimes we all need a Bitch to speak the truth to us and refocus our energy on the organization, rather than our own self-interests.

I know that I cross that thin line at times and am a Cupcake or Bitch. Sometimes it's intentional. But at my best, I widen the line. I create a place where I can stand – not on a balance beam – but on a wide road. When this balance is achieved, I feel empowered with the capacity to remain on course, and to not be sidetracked by excessive emotion, impostor syndrome, aggressive force, or timidity.

The thin line isn't just an analogy defining a strategy for women leaders to employ – it's a real dynamic that you will encounter on a daily basis. You lean too far into Bitch mode and you're ostracized. You come off as a Cupcake that's "too sweet" for a leadership position and your career stalls. Maybe your concern shouldn't be overcorrecting to one side of the thin line or the other but widening the line altogether to support the coexistence of that Cupcake AND that Bitch.

Chapter 10
P.O.W.E.R.

I **usually get an** enthusiastic "YES!" whenever I talk to women about the concept of the thin line between Cupcake and Bitch. So many women across a wide variety of sectors in the workforce seem to have experienced this dynamic but may not have considered words as illustrative as cupcake and bitch to describe it. While many women recognize the line between these two common ways to react and lead, do we straddle the line? Walk it like a tightrope? Or, try to erase it altogether?

I propose that we widen the line. Women should stand on their own two feet and determine for themselves if they jump to the Cupcake side of the line or the other – or if standing in the middle is the most effective and authentic way for them to lead. But to accomplish this, men and women alike must recognize that female leaders often confront frustrating gender bias and discrimination. Once we recognize that the playing field is not equal, we can work together to change it.

Men are important in this fight against gender bias because they usually hold the majority of the power within many organizations, including private industry, public policy-making bodies, the news media, and even religious institutions. Ignoring their power and not trying to leverage it – or simply being mad about it – is foolish.

The Lean In Foundation's 2019 Women in the Workplace Report conducted by McKinsey & Company got it right when it said, "In order to reach true equality, changing the numbers is not enough. Companies also need to invest in creating a strong culture." The report also illuminated a fact not discussed enough — all women's experiences are not the same. Other factors of a woman's identity, including their sexual orientation, physical abilities, race and religion, may be a factor in experiences with bias and discrimination. The Women in Workplace Report observes from its surveys that women of color, non-heterosexual women, and women with disabilities are having a more notably worse experience at work, receiving less support and seeing fewer opportunities to advance.

Women are not monolithic, and we are not all cut from the same block of stone. We are not uniform and equal even among each other. And, as the Lean in Foundation's report underscores, we take up space in different ways. That reality leads us to experience bias and discrimination differently. My goal here is to recommend strategies to combat gender inequity based on my own experiences and observations. I recognize the thin line between Cupcake and Bitch that I experience is different than the line women of color experience. It is my intention to suggest broad strategies to widen that line for all women across all sectors of employment. Specific tactics associated with those strategies may differ for women of color, lesbians, bisexual women or women with disabilities.

I don't often quote comedians, but when I listened to Charlie Rose interview Steve Martin in 2015, Steve's advice was spot on. During the interview, Steve was asked for his advice about making it in show business. He replied that you have to "be so good they can't ignore you." Even though this advice was directed at aspiring actors and comedians, it's transferrable to any profession and to a wide cross-section of women.

So, HOW can you be so good they can't ignore you? What do you add to your skill set arsenal to widen the thin line between Cupcake and Bitch? Women should have strategies to use when faced with work situations that are challenging and steeped in gender bias. These tactics and strategies can lessen the effects of bias and discrimination and widen the thin line.

I've given these strategies an acronym to help us remember what to do. It's P.O.W.E.R.: Preparation. Ownership. Wisdom. Energy. Respect.

"P" is for Preparation

There's simply no substitute for preparation. The other elements of P.O.W.E.R are less effective at widening the thin line without the hard work of preparation. This aspect of P.O.W.E.R. requires the emotional intelligence to be honest about your blind spots. Maybe you know you don't always prepare enough for meetings. In that case, you should carve out time on your calendar to focus on the meeting's agenda and objectives you need to accomplish. Preparation also requires self-discipline to focus on tasks you don't enjoy. Perhaps you have a desire to climb the ladder at your organization and take on management responsibilities, but you are not comfortable with conflict. If that example sounds familiar, then keep reading – we'll cover that in the next chapter. Unresolved blind spots can trip up even the most experienced leader.

Unfortunately, I saw this lack of preparation play out for one of my friends. He was asking for the Mayor's endorsement in a local race, and I brought him in for an interview. I knew he was well-versed in pertinent policy issues, but his interview was abysmal. He couldn't answer basic questions about how he would implement his public policy objectives and couldn't articulate any meaningful vision. When he learned he didn't get the Mayor's endorsement, he called me that evening claiming I betrayed our friendship. Apparently, he thought our friendship would get him what he wanted without any preparation on the substance of the topics. That's not how I do business.

One of the more disappointing aspects of this story is that he would have been a great public servant. His heart was in the right place, and he would have been a staunch supporter of diversity and inclusion efforts. He truly would have helped widen the line for women in his orbit. His lack of preparation sabotaged his chances and it was no one's fault but his own.

Another friend of mine ran unsuccessfully for an elected office in November 2016. She was well-connected and knew the issues well but didn't put in the campaign work needed. She didn't want to raise money so her ability to communicate with voters through direct mail and digital ads was limited. She also had a fear of public speaking and rather than working on becoming more comfortable with a microphone, she just didn't do it. These are not good strategies for winning an election.

We debriefed after her loss, and I was disappointed with what I heard from her. She was blaming the toxic political environment for her loss. She said because she was a black woman and running on the same ballot as Donald Trump hurt her chances of winning. For years, the two of us discussed the concept of the thin line between Cupcake and Bitch, and she pointed to her election as a case study about that line. But it wasn't that simple. It was that her lack of preparation for her campaign and half-hearted effort that prevented her campaign from ever taking off at all. Blaming gender and racial bias for her loss was disingenuous. And though it gave her something to blame other than herself, she didn't learn important lessons about her own blind spots through the experience.

It's unhelpful to blame bias and discrimination as reasons why you've not succeeded when you haven't put in the work you needed to. We make it more difficult to widen the line between Cupcake and Bitch when we don't do the hard work of preparation. That behavior does nothing to break down societal and institutional barriers that keep bias and discrimination intact.

"O" is for Ownership

Once you've done the work to prepare, own the situation at hand. Executive presence, as we've already discussed, is a big part of this. Overcoming impostor syndrome also helps with ownership.

Owning your own goals is a key, but often overlooked, component to widening the line between Cupcake and Bitch. Beware of the inclination to adopt other people's goals as your own as this tendency usually instigates impostor syndrome. Get clear on what it is that you're after and build a plan to achieve it.

A young woman in the Mayor's Office was responsible for communicating the mayor's agenda and the city's brand to the public. Her work product began steadily declining over time, and I started to see that she was a negative influence on her colleagues' productivity and morale. When I addressed this with her, she immediately burst into tears and admitted that she felt out of place in our organization. "I'm never going to be you. I don't like politics, and I don't even want to try and understand the details of the negotiations you're in the middle of. This just isn't for me," she said. I was unable to get her to understand that I didn't need her to be like me or anyone else. She didn't even need to have an interest in the minutiae of the public policy projects going on around her. We needed her to use her creativity to communicate our agenda effectively. That was her gift, and she needed to reframe her own goals around her own skills.

We are all better able to reach our goals when we own our talents and interests. One young man I worked with in the Senator's office was particularly skilled in public speaking and communicating complex ideas. He flirted with the idea of running for office right after college graduation. After some reflection, and consultation with others, he realized his gift was not in fundraising at that point in his career. He also realized that he would be a more effective leader with some additional experience. Rather than running for office that year, he became a spokesperson for a think tank in Washington, D.C., and continued in that role for a decade. He then returned to North Carolina and won an election for County Commissioner in 2008.

You also must own YOUR definition of success and failure. In politics, people tend to define their successes by the ballot box. Sometimes you can lose an election, but still move an issue forward.

I can remember an interview with Hillary Clinton after her loss to Donald Trump in 2016. She admitted she was devastated over losing the electoral college vote count. But after 2016, scores of women were motivated to start their own campaigns and run for elected office in their communities. Hillary Clinton said that watching women become leaders was a different type of sweet victory.

This dynamic can also play out in the board room. Managers can often set success and failure measures for their employees based on quantitative data alone, like sales. However, it's also important to consider factors like brand growth when contemplating how successful a project is. Whether it's brand growth or the professional growth of an employee, forward movement and success can be as important as reaching an established numerical goal.

I saw an example of this when a Kansas City-based Fortune 500 company broadcast its news about record-shattering profits during one quarter. During the next quarter, they made impressive strides at increasing diversity in their C-suite. However, there was no press release or happy hour celebrating that achievement. This didn't sit well with many employees. It made them feel as if the only important type of success involved increasing the bottom line. It was a missed opportunity for the company to help set a different standard for success.

I also encourage men to take ownership when it comes to widening the thin line between Cupcake and Bitch. Too often a woman is left to defend herself against bias. It's one thing for a woman to call out a man for biased behavior. It's another for men to use their power and privilege to push back on other men's inappropriate, biased behavior.

Late nights are normal for staffers working in the Missouri State Capitol from January until May. One night several of us, two women and three men, were waiting for the Senate to vote on a contentious bill. A young woman in her first session as a legislative aide was with us and asked a question about the voting procedure. One of the male state representatives said, "God, I'm glad you're pretty." Her question may have been basic to anyone with any legislative experience, but she was just learning the ropes. And his reaction was childish, distasteful, and demeaning.

Two men witnessed that and snickered. Neither came to her defense by putting the state representative in his place. I paused, waiting for one of the guys to say something – anything. I felt like their rebuke of his behavior would have more of an impact than mine would. I knew them all well and also knew they would be livid if anyone spoke to their daughters that way. But while I paused, the bell rang for the voting to start, and everyone got up and left. I had waited too long to chastise the representative for his inappropriate behavior. The young woman sat there in tears. I promised myself that if I witnessed something like that again, it was up to me to point out gender discrimination and harassment.

"W" is for Wisdom

Gaining wisdom about yourself, other people, and different situations and systems can help you leverage your P.O.W.E.R. You can get this wisdom from a book, a network of people, and managing through positive and negative experiences. Wherever you get it and whatever wisdom it is, you have to put into action. What's the point of gaining of wisdom if you sit on it?

Here is a cautionary piece of advice: I used to think that every piece of wisdom I'd ever need would come from a book. Maybe it's because I hadn't been exposed to many people with a formal higher education, or maybe I was just ignorant about the value of life experience. There have been many times throughout my career when I developed a strategy to get out of a difficult situation because I had already been in similar situations. No book provided a blueprint. I learned by listening, watching, and soaking up the expertise, and sometimes the failures, of others.

Wisdom does tend to arrive hand-in-hand with experience. The more often you've been in a high-profile political communications crisis, the less likely you are to lose your cool when the next one comes around. The more million dollar deals you've observed or brokered, the less likely you are to flub the next one or let impostor syndrome set in. You feel more confident because it's not new territory.

Being in the presence or under the direction of poor leadership gives us wisdom as well. It's important to use your experience and emotional intelligence in these situations to learn the lessons that could be right in front of you. I've watched elected officials at every level treat civil servants as if they were beneath them. Not only does this illuminate their poor leadership and values, but it is self-defeating. City Hall staff, in particular, were critically important to our administration's success. They would proactively bring issues to us that they knew needed to be addressed. Many of those issues would have never registered on our radar. Leadership is a team sport. Learning what NOT to do from those who fail to get this important point is beneficial wisdom to take on your leadership journey.

"E" is for Energy

Bitches and Cupcakes both need energy to keep moving. It's important to determine what things, people, and places give you energy. As needed, turn to them to energize yourself. There's no shame in taking care of yourself. I've also identified two different strategies for staying energized. The first is to dump toxic people, and the second is to limit the non-promotable tasks that seem to fall your way.

Finding the strength to let go of toxic relationships is freeing and healthy. We all know these relationships. They can be with colleagues who are manipulative, acquaintances who are overly negative, or family members who take far more than they give. Many of us simply don't – or can't – end those relationships. We often fail to manage the time we spend with those individuals because we feel some sort of pressure to keep them in our orbit.

But their toxic behavior is sapping our energy. We give ourselves the space to re-energize and focus on our own productivity and happiness when we limit or let go of these unhealthy relationships.

I supervised a woman who, from the beginning, was not a great fit for our organization, but I felt compelled to help her fit in because we needed her skill set. Despite repeated attempts to give her professional development and one-on-one coaching, she only became more and more toxic to the office. She distracted her colleagues from their work, she exacerbated personality clashes among our staff, and she consistently struggled to maintain our pace. It also became painfully obvious over time she had unrealistic expectations of her role. She was absent when we needed a strategic thinker to help navigate complex issues. But you could count on her being present for events involving photo shoots and light-heartedness. She was manipulating her position for her own entertainment and benefit.

Being around her became a chore. Managing her was something even worse. When coaching and professional development didn't help her work product or her attitude, we both agreed our organization was no longer a good fit for her. When she told me she was moving on, I was relieved that her toxicity would be coming to an end. Team players look for ways to move their organizations' missions forward. They don't become a distraction from the mission.

I was friends for almost a decade with a woman who turned everything into something negative. She was truly a "half-empty-glass" kind of person. She had a knack for making every situation about her, too. She tended to surround herself with people who wouldn't necessarily push back on her negative behavior. She seemed to need their attention, and they were willing to give it.

I couldn't find the energy to spend time with her anymore and started avoiding her calls. Being around her had grown so exhausting that I would make up a reason not to meet her. This often made me feel guilty, and I chastised myself for being a bad friend. But after Vivian was born, I recognized I had to be more selfish with my time.

My free time decreased substantially when she arrived and what little free time I did have needed to be especially fulfilling.

Making a decision to let the friendship lapse would be difficult, as I believe it is for many women. But one evening I met her for happy hour and wanted to leave within a half-hour. She angrily recounted every small issue she had dealt with that day and everyone she considered had crossed her. Every single thing was a crisis, and, in her perspective, she was the victim in all of it. I decided right then my time and energy were too precious to spend with that negative behavior any longer. I now see her once or twice a year in very limited doses. I still care for her, but I realize that I can't let her toxic behavior occupy my mind or take me away from my priorities.

Getting sucked into non-promotable tasks can be as toxic as negative people. These tasks include – but are not limited to – planning parties, taking notes, and making copies. The difficulty with these tasks is that getting them done is completely necessary. *Legacy* is a book that details the journey of the All Blacks, a New Zealand rugby team, who went from a rock-bottom record to the most successful team in sports history. The author, James Kerr, offers readers a very powerful lesson about leadership: "Champions do extra. They sweep the sheds." This is absolutely true.

However, the problem is that women are typically the ones doing the equivalent of "sweeping the sheds" in their organizations. These non-promotable tasks can eat away at valuable time. And they don't usually help grow a person's skill set or prove that they can manage anything high-profile or contentious. They also play into impostor syndrome by reinforcing a woman's insecurities that she is only qualified to plan parties, take notes and make copies.

Several years ago, we were all gathered in the kitchen area of the Mayor's office when Sly started unloading the dishwasher. Four different female staffers jumped up to take over. The men sat there. He was setting an example, but the guys didn't quite catch on. Sly had not read *Legacy*, but he said something about how it wouldn't hurt him to do dishes, and besides, not even the Mayor is above kitchen duty. A few months later, dirty dishes were again piling up on the counter. Larissa Westenkirchner, who served for all eight years as Sly's scheduler – she's earned a special place in heaven for that – often found herself doing these dishes. She must have picked up one coffee cup too many, when she said to the team, "Your mother doesn't work here. Clean up your own shit." She was not one to express herself this way, so the element of the unexpected made an impact.

Limiting non-promotable tasks is not always easy, depending on the size of your team. However, it's good for everyone to spread these tasks around as much as they practically can. A partner at a law firm can "sweep the sheds" from time to time as well as any paralegal.

Take some time to reflect on your own organization. Who typically has the duty of planning birthday lunches, making copies, taking notes, or coordinating conference calls? If the same person does all of these tasks, then make a plan to spread those around. That could include creating a calendar for each team member to take turns as note-taker for your staff meeting. Or maybe everyone can take one week a month to make their own copies, so the person who normally does it can spend that time focused on their own professional development.

"R" is for Respect

Grandma Chamblee would tell me that if I didn't respect myself then I shouldn't expect anyone else to respect me. Respecting all the dimensions of yourself – from organizational leader and wife to mom and best friend – will give you the backbone to overcome impostor syndrome and stay centered when faced with bias and adversity. It will also help you widen the thin line between Cupcake and Bitch because respecting yourself helps protect your confidence from negative influences and gendered criticisms.

Self-respect means living your values and having the integrity to do the right thing when no one is watching. Self-respect can be learned – and improved. Not all of us are born with it or have as much of it as we need. My own self-respect has improved as I've gained more confidence in my abilities and accepted my weaknesses.

Respecting others is the basis for forming networks that can broaden your perspective, and ultimately, help you become a better leader. Approaching everyone with respect, until they give you a reason to take it back, is necessary to develop meaningful relationships.

Let's be real – not everyone may respect you in return. Then what? First, remain calm and remember that you can't control other people's actions, but you can control your reaction to them. You may be "too much" for some people or they may not see the value you bring to the situation. And then some people don't like anyone who isn't their mirror image. None of this is your problem. It's theirs. Unfortunately, not everyone you encounter will deserve your respect.

The political consultant in "Country Dumb" was a person who lost my respect. For years, he hovered over our administration with a critical eye, casting judgment on every move we made. He'd call me numerous times in the evening or on weekends if I didn't return his first phone call quickly enough. He always had an opinion, a better idea, and a condescending tone. He treated my male colleagues similarly, but I got a heightened version of his behavior. He took credit for work other people did. We also believed he leaked information to the media and our opponents.

For the first several years of our administration, I thought I had to tolerate all of this because of his institutional knowledge and his connections. He certainly made it seem his knowledge was indispensable. But eventually, I came to see that what he framed as valuable expertise was actually manipulative behavior. I also realized that he didn't respect anyone else because his own ego wouldn't allow it. I stopped returning his phone calls in the spring of 2017 and never regretted it.

Combining the elements of P.O.W.E.R. and implementing them in your professional life can help widen the thin line between Cupcake and Bitch that many women walk down. Men and women alike have a role to play in taking action on this front. The good news is that all of the components of P.O.W.E.R. – Preparation, Ownership, Wisdom, Energy and Respect – can be built and strengthened. The next step, and it's not easy, is this: It's up to us to channel our individual P.O.W.E.R. to create change in our communities. That takes sustained commitment from all of us – men and women – to take action, drive change, and gets results. Incorporating P.O.W.E.R. may be easy to do for a day. The challenge is turning one day into a daily lifestyle.

Chapter 11

Navigating *Conflict* While Female

$\mathcal{T}$**hroughout my career,** I've noticed that women in many professions tend to be missing from situations involving conflict. I've often wondered if institutional and systemic bias create conditions where women are left out of these situations. Or perhaps it's impostor syndrome again – that feeling that we can't possibly manage a conflict if we aren't the subject matter expert. In reality, it's a combination of all of these factors that is likely to blame for the lack of women leading organizations out of conflict.

This can lead to gender inequity at the top because individuals in leadership positions usually face some conflict when managing people, making decisions and leading through change. Conflict is part of the natural cycle of leadership. If women are going to take on more leadership positions in the C-suite, in government and in our communities, then we must grow our management skills.

A solution for conflict may seem elusive when voices rise and dissenting opinions are met with dismissal. We can achieve better results by focusing on executive presence, specifically communicating authority and keeping emotions in check.

Communicating authority is paramount when navigating conflict. Both colleagues and superiors consciously and unconsciously questioned my authority because of my five-foot-tall stature, southern drawl, and gender. This is a big reason why I'm such a believer in all three components of executive presence: physical appearance, verbal and nonverbal communication, and emotional control.

I observed how one colleague, who surpassed everyone else in the room in subject matter expertise, became useless in developing a compromise policy plan in a situation wrought with conflict, because her emotions and feelings got in the way. She lacked something, and it wasn't an education or experience. That "something" was an ability to manage her own passion on the issue in order to lead the group toward a pragmatic solution.

Another colleague failed to develop a compromise on a major management issue for her company because she had already made up her mind about the end result she wanted. Her bias on the issue and inflexibility made her ineffective in building consensus. In the end, her credibility was tarnished, and she was replaced in the conflict setting with someone who could be more objective.

Both of these women had a mastery of the subject matter and a strong passion for how the outcome should look. However, they struggled to blend the two and were unable to be as effective as they needed to be. It's necessary to honestly consider your own objectivity when you're developing a compromise on an issue that you're passionate about. Watch out for red flags that can help you determine if you're passionate about the outcome or if you're biased. Passion is a strong emotion that can be kept in check, but bias can be detrimental to moving an issue forward. You can determine if there are red flags by considering the following questions:

- Do you want to see a compromise, or are you holding out to get what you want?
- Can you visualize a satisfying end result that includes you moving away from your current position?
- Do you reject the other side's ideas and opinions without truly considering their merits?
- Can you articulate why your position should be considered based on pertinent facts and data, and not on emotion?

- Finally, can you articulate the other side's position without adding your opinion? This helps you keep their goals in mind. If you understand the goals of the other team's opinion, then you can clearly find common ground between their objectives and yours.

I'm reminded of the advice from the North Carolina Senator: "I can be bitter and pissed at the world when I'm underestimated because of my personal presence, or I can use their underestimation to my advantage." This has really proven true. And as much as I genuinely hate to admit it, it's usually not a matter of if, but when, women in leadership roles will have their authority and their expertise questioned. Your own self-awareness and self-actualization in connection with how you'll be perceived and react is critical. I have yet to see anger and vitriol help these frustrating moments, though they indeed may be warranted.

While I was the Mayor's Chief of Staff, I winced more than once watching a city councilwoman's behavior during tense negotiations and public hearings. She had a penchant for shaking her finger at staff, raising her voice at her own constituents, and eve ᴏrming out of a room if things weren't going her way. A female intern approached me after one of her outbursts and said, "Well, she just set the women's movement back a hundred years." The councilwoman's outburst is not the example more experienced women leaders should set for younger women. And her outrage didn't accomplish anything. Leaders – both and women – should refrain from overcorrecting in a bad situation. For women in particular, this approach does nothing to overcome other people's biases towards them. The councilwoman gave her detractors the space to continue their gendered criticisms.

We can communicate authority without being argumentative and we can be firm in our positions without being disrespectful. Bad behavior doesn't make you seem more powerful. It just makes you seem less of a leader.

Balancing Self-Image

Too many times, women are marginalized as leaders in critical moments when conflict occurs because they have not "done the work" on self-awareness. When I feel marginalized in leadership situations, I try to remind myself that I cannot change the lens through which others see me. But, more importantly, we should remember that we can manage how we see ourselves, which in turn, helps us radiate self-confidence and generates the respect of others in times of conflict. Before we can successfully navigate conflict, we must take stock of how executive presence and self-image make us who we are. The jobs we do, the lives we live, and the issues and people we value, deserve and benefit from being sold on our self-image.

Taking time to respond to the questions I've listed below will help you evaluate whether you've done the necessary work on your self-image to help you navigate conflict. If you end up with more than two "NO" responses, you may need to improve your self-image.

Do You Have Control of Your Self-Image?

Have you done the required work necessary to successfully navigate conflict while being female?

1.	Am I satisfied with my front-of-room executive presence and its impact?	YES	NO
2.	Am I comfortable with my voice?	YES	NO
3.	Am I comfortable in my role as a leader?	YES	NO
4.	Do I adopt a natural, comfortable posture?	YES	NO
5.	Is my personal brand consistent with my presence?	YES	NO

When you watch a strong positive leader – a person who exudes confidence during conflict – what you're witnessing is his or her executive presence, a combination of competencies conveying credibility, and translating their skills into influence and respect. Not even executive presence can eliminate conflict, but it does help avoid being run over.

If we are not confident as women in our self-image, then we have little ability to hold our heads high, look people in the eye, and execute a strategic approach to navigate conflict. The end result: all of our subject matter expertise is of little use. Even smart, hardworking professionals can fail to evaluate and own their self-image, and therefore omit this requirement for leading and navigating conflict.

A female CEO of a Fortune 500 company walked into a room of business leaders who had all gathered to vote on the direction of the Chamber of Commerce's legislative agenda. I knew she felt strongly about education issues while most of the others wanted to focus on economic development incentives. The male CEOs were carrying the conversation, and she seldom added her voice and perspective to the discussion. When the meeting adjourned, she hadn't even pushed her stance. The other participants didn't even have the chance to hear her arguments because she didn't try to make her point. In the end, she voted for the economic development priorities. When I asked her about this, her response floored me. "I just assumed if everyone else felt so strongly then they were right, and I was wrong." I couldn't believe an accomplished CEO had such poor self-confidence. Her self-image prevented her from defining herself as a leader in that room. Self-image and self-confidence are connected.

Whether I am speaking on the platform to hundreds of people, or facing down a local news camera, I easily find myself wishing I was taller and didn't have a southern drawl. However, those clearly aren't aspects of my identity that I can change, so I try to resist letting what I'm "not" define my self-image. Instead, I strive to establish my persona as one that commands respect – from the clothes I wear to the way I sit in a chair. As cliché as it is, my personal presence comes from being comfortable with my self-image and at ease with who I am.

Successfully navigating conflict while female starts with owning your own image and style. Petite, female with a southern accent who throws around some colorful language – these are outward descriptions of me. Organizational leader, respected communicator, seasoned negotiator, educated thought leader – these are my internal pillars. I work very hard to make sure these internal pillars come into focus within sixty seconds of entering a room.

Control Trigger Words and Know Your Boiling Points

For me, expanding the thin line starts with word choices. Some words and phrases are emotionally charged and trigger me or others. Other words are more neutral. In every conflict, I need to know those trigger words, and I need to have alternatives on the tip of my tongue. Trigger words or phrases can halt progress quickly in a negotiation. They can make people put up walls and shut down any inclination to compromise by eroding goodwill.

One such trigger phrase is "You people." I've heard this phrase with its racial undertones uttered many times in a variety of situations. It's usually something like, "You people don't get it." I witnessed this trigger phrase cause significant damage to some key relationships for the North Carolina Senator. A political consultant from Washington, D.C., was filming a television commercial for the Senator. We were setting up the background in a tobacco field, complete with extras like farmers in overalls and cute kids in pigtails. The consultant was in the middle of a negotiation with three leaders of the Hispanic community about whether they would appear in the commercial and voice support for the Senator. They wanted guaranteed face-to-face interaction with the Senator before they agreed to being in the commercial. The consultant fired back, "You people need to get your egos in check." All three of the Hispanic leaders walked back to their vehicles without any further discussion. It took months for the Senator's staff to rebuild that relationship.

Rather than using trigger words and phrases that instinctively make individuals retreat to their respective positions, try using words reflecting commonalities and create a feeling of togetherness. For example, rather than saying, "You are seriously about to blow this whole negotiation," consider repositioning to, "We all have worked hard to get this far. Let's continue to focus on agreement points and get this thing settled."

Fuses tend to short-circuit as conflict escalates. When emotion overrides rational thought, beware a crisis may be brewing. Your body will send early warning signs, some strong and others very subtle. These warning signals can include increased heart rate; sweaty palms; shallow and rapid breathing; heat-flushed face; throat constriction; or a tightened neck or jaw. These sensations will feel uncomfortable, if not intolerable. If you begin feeling any of these symptoms, STOP! Take a moment to take several deep breaths. Seek some honest reflection time and consider the following common boiling points with a neutral party. These five points, if not managed, can increase hostilities and significantly decrease the likelihood of a compromise.

Boiling Point	Possible Solutions
Half-Truths	Affirm the half of the statement that is true and learn to delay the half that is false.
Losing Control	The best way to avoid being caught off guard is to never be on the guard. Take time to find ground that's safe and stand there.
It Got Personal	Don't personalize the event. Work hard to stay above the fray. Accusations, threats, and hostility may feel aimed at you, but they're not

I've Gotta Save This	Let people work through issues. It is so easy to jump in, save and protect. In many cases, that is not your role.
Rushed Timelines	Force thinking, not solutions. Rushing to a resolution could exacerbate boiling points and until the solution is owned, you are not done. Let discussions play out. It forces communication and clarity.

I know that one of my boiling points is facing intellectually dishonest arguments. I find it extremely difficult negotiating with individuals whose only arguments are based on protecting their turf and personal interests.

Intellectually dishonest arguments were plentiful during negotiations over our Pre-K plan. Educators told the media that the Mayor's Office hadn't consulted them when drafting the plan. But, in fact, we had engaged them for several years, even taking the majority of their suggestions. I told one superintendent that not getting everything he wanted was not the same thing as never having a conversation.

On another occasion, we came to an impasse on the definition of a school voucher. Broadly speaking, a voucher system allocates fewer dollars to the K-12 public school system and instead gives that money to private schools. Kansas City's Pre-K instruction is overwhelmingly given by community-based providers, including religious institutions, not the public schools. School districts already gave funding to community-based providers since the districts didn't have the capacity to provide pre-school instruction to every child who needed it. The Mayor's plan would have an independent institution making funding decisions, rather than allowing the public school districts to control funding. When asked the difference in that system and the one the Mayor's office was proposing, one superintendent said, "Well, it's just not a voucher if we do it." This intellectually dishonest argument based in a turf war killed a plan that would have provided a better start in their academic careers to 4,600 more four-year-olds.

Recognize and Avoid Circular Arguments

Over time, I've learned to avoid to circular arguments. Unlike a logical argument, circular arguments frame the end of the disagreement to be dependent on the initial one without any proof of its validity. Here is a simple example of a circular argument: You must obey the law because it's illegal to break the law. Circular arguments are a favorite of people who haven't necessarily done the work of preparing the substance of their argument, or who don't understand the other side's viewpoint.

Circular arguments escalate through emotion-laden language and raised voices. Try using de-escalating sentences like: "I can see you each have strongly held opinions. Continuing to argue the same points of conflict is a waste of time for all of us. Let's focus on some areas of agreement." To move ahead, you have to end circular arguments.

I observed one elected official in particular try to use circular arguments to prove her point. She was heavily supported by public safety unions in her election and conveniently advocated vehemently for those interests when it came time to pass a balanced budget. She argued, "Police and fire deserve more resources because they're heroes. I'm not going to let them down!" The issue was not whether police and fire personnel were heroes – they are. The issue was whether the city could afford their budget requests.

Acknowledge the Mistakes You're Responsible For

There are times when the actions of the past show up in the form of accusations. Hurt and misunderstanding exist in these spaces. Acknowledging the past, and the mistakes you're responsible for, isn't always easy.

Accusations from either side of the table often result in defensiveness and can negatively affect consensus and destroy shared understanding of the path forward. Like trigger words, accusatory language creates a vulnerable point for many leaders. Being prepared to own the past, but not internalize it, can help you continue forward. I've found this comment helpful: "We are all here because of issues that happened in the past. Let's acknowledge previous actions didn't get us very far and move on to the next steps."

I saw this play out while managing a conflict resolution between labor union leaders and developers. We wanted the two sides to come together and find a balanced way to incorporate prevailing wage into residential and commercial development. But prior actions and attitudes kept creeping into the discussions. Unions had picketed the developers' sites when they were unhappy with working conditions and pay. The developers took a "my-way-or-the-highway" approach to dealing with the unions' concerns. This was a recipe for a stalemate in negotiations and made a comprehensive solution impossible.

Finally, we took some incremental steps in the talks and I was adamant about celebrating even the smallest steps forward. Taking the time to recognize and celebrate any forward movement can build momentum and helps push even the most strident person to continue working towards compromise. The history between the unions and developers made it difficult to strike a more sweeping agreement everyone could live with. But in spite of that, both sides left with a better understanding of how their past actions affected the present day. Considering where the situation began, this was a major victory.

Don't Let 'Em Catch You Clueless

Through the years, I've learned to always be prepared. There's a correlation between my lack of preparation and my high-tension level when friction and conflict happen. When I'm ill-prepared, I'm more tense and more likely to become defensive. If you want the best outcome, you need to do the heavy lifting of preparation. As Grandpa Chamblee would say, "Don't let them catch you clueless."

People and issues can, and have, blown up in my face. Below are six questions I've found helpful to ask myself before negotiations or potentially contentious meetings. Preparing the responses ahead of time focuses my energy and thoughts on finding a solution, rather than on my emotions and the personalities involved. And I always remind myself, "Listen first and talk second!"

Preparing For Potential Conflict During Negotiations
- Do I know the minimum/maximum expectations for the outcome?
- Are there gaps in the information I have? If so, find the answers.
- Do I know the most likely position of each party?
- Have I identified triggers and non-negotiables?
- Can I start with a middle ground where all parties agree?
- What does success look like for each of the parties involved?

Conflict can be unpredictable, and you'll inevitably need to pivot to account for unforeseen circumstances. This is all the more reason to prepare for the parts of conflict that you can, before you ever step foot in the room.

Watch for the Opposition's Alliances

Politics exist in every organization; it's not a concept confined to government. Politics and conflict make strange bedfellows. In many cases the work or pressures of conflict happen outside the walls of the meeting – the notorious "meeting after the meeting." I cannot tell you how many times I've been caught unaware of agreements made, sometimes under the table, before we even discussed an issue. As you prepare for events, focus on these surprise alliances or unseen affiliations that can surface. Here are four possible alliances that the opposition may have formed:

- Relationships that create power blocks and may promote bullying for a specific purpose. You may need to "even the odds" to ensure fair discussion.
- Clock-watchers may use the time to delay or to create undue pressure for a solution. If it's your meeting, do not let clock-watchers control your agenda or discussions.
- Single-issue positioning: the opposition has come to the table with only one thing on its agenda and doesn't take the totality of the situation into consideration.
- Gatekeepers: This alliance has come to protect the status quo.

These four alliances can be managed, but only if you thoroughly prepare for the possible implications of each one. Preparation opens your eyes and mind – with the added benefit of helping you to keep calm.

Navigating conflict takes practice, and your experiences will be memorable and a part of the learning process. While each situation may be different, similarities will exist. If conflict arises, it doesn't mean you've failed. Remember, there's no change without conflict, and nearly every person has an incentive to change direction. It's your job to find out what that incentive may be. In my experience, we don't always find that incentive until we're "in the moment" of conversation and negotiation. That's where resiliency and adaptability – a couple of the key leadership traits discussed earlier in this book – are crucial.

While being the Cupcake or the Bitch can be effective in managing conflict, sometimes neither is optimal. I've come to understand I diminish my value in conflict settings if I'm worried about either side of the line. Rather, I focus on bringing the best version of my leadership skills to the situation, based on the dynamics in front of me.

The Best Defense is a Good Offense

Have you ever received a compliment and within moments you realized it was a slight, a dig, a snide comment, or even worse, a dreaded passive-aggressive remark? While Chief of Staff, I was engaged in a high-profile dispute where all parties walked away from the meeting feeling good. One participant told me, "You were 'surprisingly calm,' even when things got really heated." Perhaps he meant this as a compliment, but what I heard was, "It surprised me you didn't screw it up and get all emotional and illogical!"

Until that moment, I felt accomplished about my work during the meeting. But now, a part of me wanted to use this hard-won confidence and snap back with a pithy response to let him know I understood the underlying implication of his remark.

I stood squarely in front of him, and from a full foot below his six-foot-high eye level, I smiled and said, "You're right, I didn't screw up. And, yes, I'm a woman, too." He looked at me with a puzzled stare and I said, "You don't get it, do you?" Telling him this felt good. No regrets, I thought at the time.

Wrong. On my drive home that evening, I kept wondering if I had put a good outcome at risk.

He called me a few days later and said, "I get it now. You knew what you were doing, and that made me uncomfortable. I don't understand the discomfort I felt, but I know I was wrong." He thanked me for helping his organization get what they were hoping for, and we hung up the phone.

I was glad I had owned my reaction instead of softening it. Even better, I didn't impulsively apologize or take it back when he called. Do I have doubts before or after these types of situations? Sure. However, confronting – or calling out -- bias or inequitable inclinations helps stop the doubting. When I'm working through a conflict, I make sure my reactions clearly communicate, "I am an expert, a professional, and I know what I'm doing." Navigating conflict and situations like this calls upon leveraging the P.O.W.E.R we discussed in the previous chapter.

When Cupcake and Bitch Collide While Navigating Conflict

I was asked to negotiate consensus on a thorny issue, where several stakeholders considered themselves experts, but didn't hold me in the same regard. One stakeholder asserted that I couldn't possibly be qualified to be at the table. Adrenaline flooded through me. I felt defensive. Prepared and ready, I said, "You're right, I am not a subject-matter expert, but I have led more successful political and policy campaigns than everyone at the table combined. I clearly know how to package a bold vision. That's what we need here." The dynamic changed after that, and while we didn't become instant friends, the group managed to continue our discussions in a more respectful and effective way.

Cupcake? Probably not. I widened the line. I made my point and we moved ahead. That's what navigating conflict while female is about – bringing people together, removing barriers, and being empowered as a positive force to drive change.

Recognizing that women leaders still don't have an equal playing field, understanding the dynamics of the world in which they find themselves every single day, and thinking through behaviors to help – and those that don't – are how we can make that unlevel playing field more even.

Chapter 12
Where's the Good Ol' *Girls' Club*?

It **was about** 5:30 on a beautiful Friday afternoon in Raleigh during the spring semester of my senior year of college. I found myself in need of career advice, so I decided to join some of my colleagues from the Senator's office for happy hour. They always sat at the same corner table at a downtown bar within walking distance from the office. This Friday afternoon happy hour was a regular event, so I assumed I could stop by, have a drink, and chat. But when I took a seat, all four of them – guys – gave me a bewildered look. "The girls from the office don't usually come here," one guy said.

Despite the awkward start, we eventually had a robust discussion about politics, business, and networking. One of the more interesting insights from the conversation was the fact that the women in the office rarely came to those happy hours. It seemed bizarre to me. On Monday I asked all three of the women in our office – out of a seventeen-member staff – why they didn't go to happy hour on Friday afternoons. They all said that by Friday afternoon they simply didn't have the energy to network or build relationships. Maybe it was the pressure of social norms and biases catching up with them. Or perhaps it was the fact that their family responsibilities were waiting for them – the infamous "second shift" – at home and the men on our staff didn't feel the same type of burden. Either way, the women said their only goal on Friday evenings was to retreat to their homes and not deal with the office happy hour. "And that's why the good 'ol boys' club continues," one female colleague told me. "The women are just too busy and exhausted to add something else to their plates."

So, where's the good 'ol girls' club? And I don't just mean Friday happy hours. Rather, where are the sustained, effective support strategies among women that help dismantle stereotypes and social norms, knock down biases, and build more women leaders? How can we ensure we're all on the same team and serve as a collective support system for each other?

First, let's refocus our attention away from "climbing the career ladder" and towards building a permanent framework for those women behind us and around us. Climbing a ladder is great, but eventually, it's folded up and put back in the garage until it's needed again to change the light bulb that's just out of reach. So instead, let's focus on building permanent steps of a staircase. Like a ladder's rungs, each stair helps us rise to places we might not have been able to reach. Women need more permanent steps in order to make lasting progress and leave behind stereotypes and bias. Here are a few permanent steps we can walk up together.

Be Deliberate

We are more likely to achieve any goal – whether it's dismantling bias, finally writing that book, or losing those last five pounds – if we are deliberate in taking action to address it. One paradigm I've always incorporated into taking action, driving change, and getting results is that activity does not equal action. Good intentions don't lead to results unless they're backed up with something more concrete.

Lots of people talk about being supportive of women. You see this in social media channels, campaign promises, and speeches by elected officials, advice from organizational management experts, and even celebrity interviews. But talk alone doesn't move the needle. And talk without action can give people false hope. It's important that we focus on careful, well-conceived strategies and tactics that improve opportunities for women.

When I became Sly's Chief of Staff in 2014, I wanted to find a way to support other women. I was determined to create concrete action steps that would make a difference.

I lost count a long time ago of all the women's leadership roundtables, seminars, symposiums, and conventions that I've attended through the years that didn't result in any change or measurable action. Kansas City's blueprint for women's empowerment was the result of several months of research, stakeholder engagement, and analysis. The blueprint included the action steps we took to support female entrepreneurs, women employees within city government, and to increase the civic participation of women throughout the city. The fact that the two men in charge, Sly, and City Manager Troy Schulte, used their power and provided the resources needed to shine a light on women's leadership and create real change sent a message to the entire community. People understood that building an inclusive culture and supporting women's leadership were priorities for the administration.

One action step that resulted in a significant change was the Appointments Project, a collaboration with the Women's Foundation, and their President and CEO, Wendy Doyle. The Women's Foundation conducts insightful research to learn more about barriers women face in civic leadership. We worked closely with them to better understand those barriers, deconstruct them, and increase the number of women serving on Kansas City's boards and commissions.

The research revealed several barriers we needed to address. First, women were not usually asked to serve. And if they were, they hesitated saying yes because they were concerned how efficiently meetings were run. Women wanted to know that their time would be used efficiently. Meeting procedures were reinforced so that everyone's time was maximized, and women were assured that they would be valuable assets to city government. Because the Mayor's office was already aware of racial disparities throughout the city, we wanted to ensure racial diversity, as well as gender diversity, with the Appointments Project.

A reporter called the office one afternoon to get an update on the progress of the women's empowerment initiative. When I told him the first appointments made through the Appointments Project were women of color, he responded with, "That's a great coincidence." "No, it's not," I responded. "It's deliberate."

In every metric where women lag behind men, the disparity for women of color is even more profound. Deliberate analysis and solutions are needed to ensure we understand the complexities of gender bias. In the case of Kansas City's women's empowerment initiative, we didn't want to intensify racial disparities as we tried to correct gender inequality.

Women, particularly those who reach leadership positions, have an obligation to be intentional about helping other women. The weight of our own daily battles with bias can be so heavy that intentionally helping other women can be forgotten or put on the backburner. There are important ways you can use your power and privilege to be an ambassador for the women around you. These are not necessarily heavy lifts but are rewarding and effective. Here are some ideas:

- Host a networking event and invite women from diverse industries who probably wouldn't meet otherwise. This not only positions you as a leader and a connector, but you'll broaden the reach of others and maybe open a door they didn't even know existed.

- Sponsor a woman in the early stages of her career if you hold a mid-to-high level position in your organization or community. Be deliberate about elevating her expertise and accomplishments to others. Too often, women don't adequately celebrate and publicize their own abilities. That's when sponsorship can play an instrumental role in making sure people in leadership positions understand how much value every woman brings to the table.

- Encourage women experiencing impostor syndrome.

We know that most impostor syndrome is complex and even the most notable, high-achieving women in society experience it. Impostor syndrome is neither a sign of weakness nor an indication of intelligence. It is, however, something we can overcome with support.

- Share ways to accommodate both professional and family obligations. It's not uncommon for women to find themselves shouldering most of the burden when it comes to taking care of children, older family members, or both. These pressures can add up to create an exhausting mental load. I'm not a fan of the term "work-life balance." To me, it seems to add an unrealistic expectation that balance can be found. I love the advice from my friend and mentor, Susan Freeman, who advises us to, "bend, flex, bob and weave" through life's obligations and responsibilities. Perfect balance is not the goal, but integrating these obligations and responsibilities feels more attainable. Sharing guidance on how we each manage this integration builds a community of individuals with empathy and appreciation for all that we attempt to juggle.

Why is this woman-to-woman support so important? Because it's easier to achieve your goals when you have a role model to show you the way. Furthermore, women who have strong relationships with other women in their profession benefit from learning from other's experiences, absorbing their counsel, and building a sense of "I'm not alone."

Don't be a Cruella de Vil

We must resist the temptation to be a Cruella de Vil. Remember her from the Disney movie, *101 Dalmations*? In this sense, Cruella de Vil types not only avoid helping other women, but they fortify barriers around other women so that they have a more difficult time climbing permanent steps. Maybe these Cruella de Vil types are insecure about their own achievements and their own place within their organization. Or maybe they lack the emotional intelligence leaders need to remove their own interests from decision-making. Whatever the case may be, this type of behavior is counterproductive and wrong.

I met a woman who was accomplished and respected in her field when I was working in Missouri state politics. She was just a few years from retirement when we met. She frequently told us "youngsters," as she referred to us, about all the barriers she was up against early in her career. It was clear she wanted us to know that she had it pretty rough. She also made it obvious she had no interest in making our paths any easier than her own. "I managed to get ahead with a lot of hard work," she said. "No one handed me a thing, and there certainly weren't other women around to guide me. You need to figure out how to make things happen on your own." After one of my female colleagues received a big promotion, the Cruella de Vil told her she wasn't ready for the position and fueled such feelings of impostor syndrome that my colleague considered leaving the organization altogether. On a different occasion, the Cruella de Vil criticized two women running for office because they would have to travel to the State Capitol five months out of the year during the legislative session. "Why would they have children if they didn't want to stick around to raise them?" she told the committee in charge of making endorsement decisions about candidates.

In another Cruella de Vil example, a woman in the legal field made it a point to undermine other women's credibility in professional settings. On one particular occasion, a large meeting with several attorneys and business leaders – mostly men – was taking place when her bad behavior was on full display. Another woman made a suggestion for the group's course of action and this Cruella de Vil replied with, "Baby girl! What made you think of that?!" Using the term "baby girl" to refer to another professional woman was demeaning and unwarranted. Her actions gave the impression she was as interested in undermining the expertise of other women at the table as she was in adding value to the conversation herself.

There is no room for any Cruella de Vil's in the fight against gender bias. It's time to switch our viewpoint to an abundant mindset rather than a scarcity mindset. A scarcity mindset traps us into thinking there is only so much opportunity and success to go around, and the world may run out of both before we get ours. On the other hand, an abundant mindset is a viewpoint that says, "There is plenty out there for everyone." In this vein, and contrary to every Cruella de Vil, the success of one woman does not take away from the success of another.

A Few Good Men

Don't worry, guys. There's a place for you alongside the good 'ol girls' club. Both men and women can help widen the thin line between Cupcake and Bitch.

All of us can use our voices when we see bias in action. Earlier in this book, I detailed a situation where men were bystanders when a young woman was humiliated. While they didn't necessarily participate in the direct action that was so unprofessional and wrong, they did participate in making the young women feel uncomfortable because they stayed silent. Silence equates to being complicit.

It's usually pretty obvious to spot harassment – inappropriate comments and wandering eyes immediately come to mind – but it can be less obvious to recognize destructive social norms because of the way we've been conditioned. The list for these destructive social norms is long, but these examples are common:

- Sitting through a meeting where a man consistently talks over a woman.

- Scheduling of networking events at times making it difficult for working parents to attend.
- Seeing women trying to lead with authenticity while being expected by others to adjust her style and "Behave like a man."
- Organizational cultures and societal expectations ignoring the demands of family responsibilities.
- Noticing that a woman was called a bitch, even though she reacted exactly like a man did in the same situation.
- Watching a woman denied a leadership position because she was assumed by decision-makers to be "too nice."

Now, think about how you'll respond in the future when these situations arise. Will you use your voice, power and privilege to deconstruct those social norms? Will you actively seek out women who need a sponsor with your network and gravitas?

If you think about the traditional good 'ol boys' club, it is both formal and informal while serving different purposes. As we build an effective response for women to the good ol' boys' club, we must consider how and why it has existed. At its root, the good 'ol boys' club protects and supports its own self-interest and existing power structures. Women could undoubtedly use a club to support their self-interests, which includes the concepts discussed in this book, like reshaping power structures, dismantling biases, building strong leadership and communications skills, and banishing impostor syndrome. However, unlike the good 'ol boys' club of the Mad Men era, the good 'ol girls' club should not forget that not every woman experiences bias in the same way.

It's time for a paradigm shift toward collective action for women while keeping in mind an abundant mindset. Yes, women are certainly better off when we work together to widen the thin line between Cupcake and Bitch so that more women find permanent steps to leadership. But society as a whole also benefits when women maximize their potential and lead.

Widening the Line: *Where* Will You Go From Here?

*J*his book has looked at the positive and negative aspects of Cupcake, Bitch, and everything in between. You've learned about tools that women – and men – can use to widen that thin line, so the remaining question to consider is where will you go from here? I've learned that sometimes in order to chart a path forward, you have to consider where you've been.

When I was growing up in rural North Carolina, women's leadership and gender bias were not topics of conversation for anyone in my orbit. I didn't see women leading companies or being elected to office. I also didn't see a network of women being deliberate about supporting other women, particularly those from a trailer park, a housing project, or those whose skin color didn't match their own. My family loved me and provided for me, but role models that could help me determine my leadership path were few and far between. I can remember telling a few family members that I had been accepted to Meredith College, and their response was, "So, you're going to get a M.R.S. degree?"

In spite of this void, I was aware of gender bias all around me. I saw women of all backgrounds shouldering the burden of staying home and raising the children, which often meant not having the choice to pursue a career. I repeatedly saw public policy decisions being made, like decreasing access to healthcare and educational opportunities, that negatively affected women. I encountered government institutions impeding the health and wellbeing of poor women and women of color. And I personally experienced low expectations from others, which fueled impostor syndrome within my own psyche.

When I first went to Meredith College, Dr. Jim Piazza, who was in the Political Studies Department, took the time to get to know my background and help me think about how I could turn my experiences and perspective into an asset. I initially had a difficult time seeing myself as successful – but he didn't. I kept thinking about the town I grew up in, and the people I had always been around. Back then, I struggled to see how I could build something different for myself that would position me for success and fulfillment. "Just because they're victims of their own time and place doesn't mean you have to be," he said. I pushed back and said I didn't really harbor negative feelings for my hometown, or the people there who lived a life that worked for them. Dr. Piazza continued, "If their worldview works for them, then leave them to it. Build a life that works for you."

When I started exploring graduate schools, Dr. Piazza counseled me to consider programs and options which would continue my education in communications, public policy, and leadership. Further developing these skills and subject-matter knowledge would position me one day as a thought leader. His motivation continued, "Think of the women you could inspire simply by being who you are – outspoken, smart, and funny." I'm grateful that I listened to him in spite of my impostor syndrome, which didn't allow me to see myself as any of those adjectives.

The more I learned about other people's viewpoints, leadership styles, communication techniques, and the political system, along with ways government could positively impact people's lives, the more I could clearly see where I wanted to go. Writing, working in government and politics, and helping women realize their leadership potential bubbled to the top of my interests.

As I started my career in politics, I noticed that the few women around me experienced a common thread – the thin line between Cupcake and Bitch. If their leadership style came off as too abrasive, then they were considered to be a bitch by both men and women within their organization. If they weren't perceived as strong enough, then they were put in the cupcake category and considered not ready for leadership. It was obvious to me that this was a dynamic men didn't face.

Even more noticeable was that both sides of the thin line between Cupcake and Bitch were constructive if used at the right time and with emotional intelligence. I've never viewed Cupcake mode or Bitch mode as wholly negative. It depends on how each mode is leveraged in a leadership situation.

The thin line between Cupcake and Bitch wasn't drawn overnight, and it's not going to widen that quickly, either. But the status quo can't continue. Throughout this book, we've discussed strategies to help widen the line at an individual level and at a societal level. Women can hone their emotional intelligence and executive presence to increase their effectiveness against biases. They can also reframe how they see themselves to tackle impostor syndrome. And men should use their power and privilege to elevate the expertise of women and help position them for success. All of us can be more deliberate about seeking diverse perspectives and taking the time to learn about different communication and leadership styles. Changes are needed at both the individual and societal levels, and one won't have as much impact without the other.

I've never believed that "man hating" helped anything. When I speak about women's leadership to audiences across the country, I always get a chuckle when I say, "I don't hate men. Quite the contrary – I've even married a couple of them."

Frankly speaking, we need men on our side if we're going to increase the number of women in leadership positions. You don't have to look too far back in history to see examples where alienating a group of people led to negativity, vitriol, and division. Men can create far-reaching conditions – like a supportive, inclusive culture within organizations – that support all women in maximizing their potential.

Men and women often have different strengths and leadership styles. Even in the late 1800s, early women's rights advocates, like Amos Bronson Alcott, noted intrinsic differences in our communication styles, "Debate is masculine; conversation is feminine," he wrote. Women should not be expected to adopt masculine leadership or personality traits in order to be effective leaders and to be respected as capable problem-solvers. The differences between men and women don't have to be problematic. The trick is to balance our strengths and find complementary ways to incorporate our different approaches to take action, drive change, and get results.

The guidance and stories within this book are intended to help both men and women think about gender bias and to recalibrate their actions and perspectives to widen that stubborn, thin line between Cupcake and Bitch. The work won't be easy, and it will take time. There are no short cuts or quick fixes. It reminds me of the work of the farmers from my childhood. Grandpa Chamblee used to say, "Changing people's way of thinking is a lot like farming. You have to start over again every morning."

Take This Action – To Get Results

You've read about everything from resiliency and impostor syndrome to executive presence and navigating conflict. Now you have the wisdom you need to widen the thin line between Cupcake and Bitch. But, as you also know, wisdom doesn't help much if you don't take action with it.

Consider the following pages part of your preparation as you build your own P.O.W.E.R. Answering the questions below will help you to identify the action steps you need to take to apply the concepts you've learned.

Chapter 1   Words You Don't Want to Hear from an Elected Official

1. Name a time when you've been underestimated. How did you deal with it and what would you do differently, if anything?

    _____

    _____

    _____

    _____

    _____

    _____

2. What's a piece of good advice you've received that you didn't expect? How did you apply it in your personal or professional journey?

    _____

    _____

    _____

    _____

    _____

    _____

    _____

3. Have you ever given unsolicited advice to someone? How should you frame your advice to ensure the recipient receives it in a constructive manner?

    _____

    _____

    _____

    _____

    _____

    _____

Chapter 2   Well, Bless Your Heart

1. Are there aspects or specific features of your background that you've considered a weakness but now view as a useful tool in your toolbox?

   _____

   _____

   _____

2. Think about a time when someone made inaccurate assumptions about you. How did you dismantle those assumptions? What would you do differently?

   _____

   _____

   _____

3. Think about a time when you realized you had formed inaccurate assumptions of someone else. How has that realization changed the way you encounter others?

   _____

   _____

   _____

Chapter 3   Country Dumb

1. How has a mentor or sponsor taught you something new or reframed your ideas about something you thought you knew?

   _____

   _____

2. Consider a mentorship relationship that you have with a mentee. What do you enjoy most about that relationship? Are there any challenges you've experienced while mentoring others? Do this same exercise while considering a sponsorship relationship.

_____

_____

_____

_____

3. Name a skills or experience gap you've had to overcome. What strategies did you use to build those skills or to gain those experiences?

_____

_____

_____

_____

4. How will you build resiliency after reading this book? Be specific.

_____

_____

_____

_____

Chapter 4   Complaints or Action: Only One Will Get Results

1. How will you interact differently with people who have "mad-at-the-world" disorder?

_____

_____

_____

_____

2. What have you learned about the type of leader you want to be? What are some avenues for you to take to turn that leadership ambition into reality?

_____

_____

_____

_____

3. What are some areas of growth in your leadership profile that you've identified? Name three tactics you'll use to focus on that growth.

_____

_____

_____

_____

_____

_____

4. How will you leverage your strengths to maximize your leadership potential?

_____

_____

_____

_____

Chapter 5   Failing Up

1. How can you play a role in shining a light on competence rather than misplaced confidence?

_____

_____

_____

_____

2.   Read through the Top Ten Leadership Lessons again. Identify one step you'll take to implement each lesson.

_____

_____

_____

_____

_____

_____

_____

_____

_____

Chapter 6   Social Norms Are the Real Bitch

1.   What is one social norm within your organization that needs recalibrating? How will you help change that norm?

_____

_____

_____

_____

2.   Can you think of a time when you engaged in self-sabotage, which played into unhelpful expectations? Consider what factors may have contributed to that self-sabotage and how you can avoid them in the future.

_____

_____

_____

_____

_____

3.   After reading this chapter, how will you use your voice to shift perceptions when confronted with bias and discrimination?

_____

_____

_____

_____

_____

_____

Chapter 7   Congrats! You May Have Something in Common With An A-Lister

1.   Think about a time when you experienced impostor syndrome. What factors do you think played into those feelings of "I don't belong here"?

_____

_____

_____

_____

_____

_____

_____

2.   What tools will you use to overcome impostor syndrome in the future?

_____

_____

_____

_____

_____

_____

3. How have you supported someone else experiencing
    impostor syndrome?

    _____

    _____

    _____

    _____

    _____

4. Practice telling your own success story. Name three
    accomplishments you're most proud of and how you
    achieved those results.

    _____

    _____

    _____

    _____

    _____

    _____

    _____

    _____

Chapter 8   Emotional Intelligence: So Important Yet in Short Supply

1. Think of a leader you observed who exhibited strong
    emotional intelligence. How did that leader inspire others
    to take action and get results?

    _____

    _____

    _____

    _____

    _____

    _____

    _____

2. Sometimes the best lessons are learned by observing poor leadership in action. List an example of poor leadership that you've witnessed and then list three ways that leader could have shown stronger emotional intelligence.

_____

_____

_____

_____

_____

_____

_____

_____

_____

3. Identify a strength and a weakness related to your:

    a. Physical presence

    _____

    _____

    _____

    b. Communications presence

    _____

    _____

    _____

    c. Emotional presence

    _____

    _____

    _____

4. How will you work on your weaknesses and build on your strengths in these three areas? Be specific and don't forget to track your milestones!

_____
_____
_____
_____
_____
_____
_____
_____

Chapter 9   Are You a Cupcake, A Bitch, or Maybe Both?

1. Give an example of when you leaned toward Cupcake mode. What worked well and what didn't? How authentic did that mode feel to you?

_____
_____
_____
_____
_____
_____
_____

2. Now repeat the exercise above for Bitch mode.

_____
_____
_____
_____
_____
_____
_____

3.   Are you comfortable exhibiting traits on both sides of the Cupcake and Bitch line? Why or why not?

_____

_____

_____

_____

_____

_____

4.   Think about a time when you perceived someone else to be in Cupcake mode. What were their behaviors that made you think they were in Cupcake mode? List a few items and then consider if your own bias played a role in your perception.

_____

_____

_____

_____

_____

_____

_____

_____

5.   Repeat exercise but switch to Bitch mode.

_____

_____

_____

_____

_____

_____

_____

Chapter 10   P.O.W.E.R.

List a growth opportunity for yourself by each element of
   P.O.W.E.R. below:

P = Preparation

_____

_____

_____

_____

O = Ownership

_____

_____

_____

_____

W = Wisdom

_____

_____

_____

_____

E = Energy

_____

_____

_____

_____

R = Respect

_____

_____

_____

_____

Chapter 11   Navigating Conflict While Female

1. What factors influence your self-image? Be honest!

_____

_____

_____

_____

_____

_____

_____

_____

_____

2. How would you rate your own executive presence? Use this scale:
    1. Needs significant improvement
    2. Needs some improvement
    3. Average
    4. Better than average
    5. Strong

3. Then, ask two people from your tribe how they would rate your executive presence. What are the similarities? The differences?

_____

_____

_____

_____

_____

_____

_____

_____

_____

Chapter 12   Where's the Good Ol' Girls' Club?

1. List three women outside your current circle whom you
    want to get to know. Be deliberate about including women
    from different races, socioeconomic backgrounds, and
    professions than yours.

    _____
    _____
    _____
    _____
    _____
    _____

2. Can you think of three men who have been champions for
    women? How can you elevate and celebrate their actions?

    _____
    _____
    _____
    _____
    _____
    _____
    _____

3. How will you react when confronted with a "Cruella De
    Vil" after reading this book?

    _____
    _____
    _____
    _____
    _____
    _____

Acknowledgements

*T*his book has been a labor of love, but even the most fulfilling tasks can take a whole tribe of support to pull off. The final touches were completed during the COVID-19 pandemic, which presented additional challenges, but also created a space for me to be perhaps more contemplative and reflective than I would have otherwise.

Teresa Sosinski and I must hold a world record for efficiently utilizing FaceTime as a means to get business taken care of. Our weekly chats, and her regular insights and edits, made me a better writer, thinker, and leader.

I'm grateful to Bob Snodgrass for publishing a book with the word "bitch" in the title and for seeing potential in this concept.

There would be no book without Sly James asking me, "What the hell are you waiting for?" His typical blunt approach to encouraging me to prioritize this book was the kick in the butt I needed to get it done.

My husband, Fred Wickham, has been extraordinarily patient and understanding while I wrote this book while I was also building a new business. As has happened more times than I care to count throughout our marriage, his desire to hang out on the couch or have a date night took a backseat to my sometimes-nauseating professional drive. He could write an entire book about how I can lean towards one particular side of the thin line. I know how lucky I am that he is so patient.

Our kids lived through this experience as well. Vivian learned to leave me alone when the home office door was closed so that I could write. The "big kids," Fred IV, Emily and Libby, served as a focus group on choosing a cover, considering chapter topics, and of course, entertained their little sister so I could write. This book is dedicated to our girls, but Fred IV deserves credit for modeling behavior that the girls should look for in any partner.

I am incredibly lucky to have a strong tribe of both men and women in my orbit. Many have been mentioned in the book, but I can't finish this project without mentioning:

My friends since childhood, Kristen Smith and Lauren Norman, have always supported my crazy ideas – from living in Russia to starting a whole new life in the Midwest to becoming an author.

Kelsey Thompson and Paula Hodges are brilliant, accomplished women who are amazing friends. I love our past, present and future.

Jim Giles has taught me so much about leadership, friendship, and life. This quote that he has repeated is a gem: "The hero comes to a point where he or she must stop worrying about what to do or how to overcome the obstacles in the way, and just do what needs to be done."

I knew I would become fast friends with Elle Hogan and Gina Stingley within ten minutes of meeting both women. Some people just click with each other. And if you're lucky, they'll read your writing, too.

And finally, my parents had a tough job raising a strong-willed, impatient, curious girl who was never satisfied with anything. Without them, my foundation would not have been as strong and following my path would have been even more difficult.

About the Authors

*J*oni **Wickham's own** journey to leadership and that thin line, began in rural North Carolina and has taken turns few people saw coming. As the daughter of a teen mother and raised in the conservative rural south, Joni was the first in her family to receive a college education and overcome the barriers of socio-economic hardship and others' low expectations of her. A native of North Carolina, Joni came to Kansas City after leading initiatives within state and federal government as well as advocacy organizations. She worked on former Kansas City

Mayor Sly James' staff and later was promoted to his Chief of Staff. Joni has proven herself to be an accomplished political strategist and negotiator, communications expert and organizational leader. She was motivated to create a first-of-its-kind women's empowerment initiative which has been implemented in several major cities.

Joni received a BA in Political Studies from Meredith College and a master's in political science from University of Missouri. She was the recipient of the 2019 Mel Carnahan Public Service Award from the University of Missouri Truman School of Public Affairs. She is the co-founder at Wickham James Strategies & Solutions. Joni lives in Kansas City with her two-legged and four-legged family.

Teresa Bruns Sosinski has written countless articles for non-profit publications and is the editor of several books for children and adults. She received a BA in English from Creighton University and is proud that her two children are as much a stickler for grammar as she is. She and her husband Dave live in New Mexico, but call Kansas City home.